Self-Directed IRAs

KIRTLEY LIBRARY
COLUMBIA COLLEGE
COLUMBIA, MO 65216

Published in cooperation with
MARKETING ONE, INCORPORATED

KIRTLEY LIBRARY

Self-Directed IRAs

*Investment, Marketing,
and Trust Administration
Strategies*

edited by Jerome R. Corsi

KIRTLEY LIBRARY
COLUMBIA COLLEGE
COLUMBIA, MO 65216

Westview Professional Handbooks on the New Banking

Westview Press / Boulder and London

332.1754
Se 48

Westview Professional Handbooks on the New Banking

This Westview softcover edition was manufactured on our own premises using equipment and methods that allow us to keep even specialized books in stock. It is printed on acid-free paper and bound in softcovers that carry the highest rating of the National Association of State Textbook Adminstrators, in consultation with the Association of American Publishers and the Book Manufacturers' Institute.

All rights reserved. No part of this publication may be reproduced or transmitted in any form or by any means, electronic or mechanical, including photocopy, recording, or any information storage and retrieval system, without permission in writing from the publisher.

Copyright © 1986 by Westview Press, Inc. Westview Press retains a copyright interest in this collection as a whole. Individual authors retain a copyright interest in their individual papers.

Published in 1986 in the United States of America by Westview Press, Inc.; Frederick A. Praeger, Publisher; 5500 Central Avenue, Boulder, Colorado 80301

Library of Congress Cataloging-in-Publication Data
Self-directed IRAs.
   (Westview professional handbooks on the new banking)
   Includes index.
   1. Self-directed individual retirement accounts.
I. Corsi, Jerome R.   II. Series.
HG1660.A3S45 1986   332.1'754   86-1679
ISBN 0-8133-7213-5

Composition for this book was provided by the editor.
This book was produced without formal editing by the publisher.

Printed and bound in the United States of America

(∞) The paper used in this publication meets the requirements of the American National Standard for Permanence of Paper for Printed Library Materials Z39.48-1984.

6   5   4   3   2   1

Westview Professional Handbooks
on the New Banking
Jerome R. Corsi, General Editor

The purpose of this series is to focus attention on emerging areas of growth in banking under deregulation. Today, banking in the United States is experiencing change at a rate unequalled since the 1930s. In the 1930s, the shift was toward making the lines separating financial industries more rigid and distinct; today, the momentum is toward eradicating those lines completely—including those barriers that divide banking and nonbanking activities and that create geographical restrictions.

Each volume will focus on a topic of industry-wide importance, featuring authors who are leading practitioners in the field. The contributors will bring their practical experience to bear on such issues as new-product development, marketing innovations, impacts on management structures, and the effects of previously unknown competition.

The series will explore the way innovations have led to a new entrepreneurial spirit and a marketing orientation in banking, an industry in which the word "sales" traditionally has been virtually ignored. The handbooks will examine the evolution in banking culture crucial to the integration of previously distinct financial disciplines such as insurance, securities, and real estate.

These practical books will include technical detail of immediate benefit to those in banking charged with innovation, as well as to those in related service industries. Spanning issues of importance to commercial banking and to the thrift industry, the series will provide continuing, practical information for those working in today's banking deregulation environment.

Other Titles in This Series

About the Book and Editor

The strong and continued demand for Individual Retirement Accounts since the enactment of the Economic Recovery Act of 1981 has surprised financial experts and created an enormous pool of investment resources. When IRA accounts were relatively small, consumers were satisfied to leave investment strategies to the vendors packaging the product, and the security of federal depository insurance provided a strong market advantage for commercial banks and savings institutions. But as accounts have grown, IRA customers have begun to consider them as their own retirement savings portfolios and are less willing to leave the investment of those funds in the hands of someone else.

Self-direction is a simple idea, yet its delivery and administration raise many complex issues. To what extent does a bank or thrift offering securities products within the self-directed IRA take on an investment advice liability? How should the self-directed IRA be constructed? The product mix offered may have to be structured to reflect varying retirement savings strategies as well as customer preference for the degree of risk/reward acceptable in this portfolio investment. The contributors to this book, who include bankers, consultants, and trust officers, as well as traditional competitors from the securities and financial planning industries, discuss the spectrum of issues affecting the self-directed account and trust administration.

Jerome R. Corsi is senior vice president, bank marketing, at Marketing One, Inc. His books include *Constitutional Law: A Political Science Casebook* and *Judicial Politics: An Introduction*.

Contents

Acknowledgments

This and the companion volume on insurance are the first two volumes in a new series of handbooks on the changes in banking amidst deregulation. The handbook series owes its existence to the creative imagination of Frederick A. Praeger, who saw the need for and the possibilities of such works. Fred, an entrepreneur himself in an established industry, grasped immediately the consequences of change in banking and the opportunity for written reflections with the intelligence of one who adds to what he is presented.

This book is based on a series of seminars held under the auspices of the Banking Law Institute operated by Executive Enterprises, Inc., a professional management education organization. Brian McGrath, president of Executive Enterprises, graciously extended to me the opportunity to organize these conferences and to select the speakers. These meetings always benefit from the skilled staff of Executive Enterprises and most especially from the work of Andrea Dolce-Singer. I could always concentrate on creating the program and chairing the meeting, knowing that every detail of announcement, preparation, and logistics could be successfully negotiated by Andrea and her staff.

The manuscripts were skillfully edited and prepared for publication by the diligent efforts of Diana Dale and Joy Corsi. Given my travel schedule during the production of these books they literally were completed only because Diana and Joy took full responsibility for every detail, including coordinating with the authors and the publisher.

The manuscript was processed on an Apple Macintosh™ Plus computer. Final copy was prepared by utilizing the following software: Microsoft® Word, Microsoft® Chart, MacDraw™, and Aldus PageMaker for Macintosh™. Camera-ready copy was produced on the Apple LaserWriter™ Plus. Diana and Joy mastered microcomputer desktop publishing to accomplish the task. At Westview Press, Susan McEachern worked with

x

Diana and Joy in production as she organized the series promotion, assisted in developing and refining the series concept, and lent a hand at editing.

My experience in this area derives from my work with Marketing One, Inc., and Marketing One Securities, Inc. John Christensen, Marketing One's corporate communications officer, assisted in making sure we had the required Apple computer equipment in Portland in time for final production and provided help in working through the intricacies of using the machines. My numerous colleagues at Marketing One have made our exploration into the world of deregulated banking one of the most enjoyable challenges of my life.

Jerome R. Corsi
Portland, Oregon

Introduction

In 1986, several factors combined to create an awareness of the need to manufacture self-directed IRA products and services:

- •While commercial banks and thrifts had enjoyed the majority of IRA deposits since 1982, interest rates were at a single-digit decade low during tax season 1986. Consumers holding double-digit yield proforma projections suffered "interest rate shock" when returning to their banks to make deposits during this time.
- •Given the accumulation of IRA deposits since 1982 and the possibility of significant lump sum deposits as rollovers from pension or other tax-qualified funds, many IRAs approached or exceeded the $10,000 threshold. Psychologically, as IRA deposits increase in size, consumers seem to undergo a transformation from viewing these deposits as safe long-term retirement nest eggs, to considering their IRAs as their own tax-deferred investment portfolio deserving of more active management.
- •The 1986 tax season proceeded amidst one of the strongest bull markets investors have enjoyed during this century.

This particular scenario could be written almost on the exact specification of events required to create an investor willingness to shift IRA deposits from the safe but sleepy depository vehicle to the more risky but seemingly more compelling investment opportunity.

Banks which entered 1986 tax season expecting a 60% market share of new IRA deposits, emerged with somewhat more in the range of 40%. With total IRA deposits expected to exceed $265 billion in 1986, the competition for the customer relationship was intensifying.

Moreover, federal deposit insurance alone is not sufficient to retain market share for depository IRAs. To compete, banks today must also compete on yield. And in this interest environment, to compete with rates would have pushed costs of funds into clearly unprofitable realms. It is no wonder the 1986 IRA season was considered "flat" by bankers. Not even the much-touted promotion of a free boat cruise or an exotic airplane ticket could answer the needs of the customer who preferred instead an extra fifty or one hundred basis points on the IRA certificate of deposit.

The push for creating a self-directed IRA became intense. For defensive reasons, some banks sought "me too" self-directed IRAs, if only to be able to block the customer on the way to the door. Some banks advertised self-directed IRAs without informing even branch managers, customer service representatives, new account representatives, or tellers that the facility existed. Had customers demanded to know what was behind the advertisements and persisted to sift through the bureaucratic maze to find the appropriate retirement savings administrator, they might have been told to go to their broker, buy the investments they want, return to the bank, at which point the bank would place the investments into an appropriate trust account.

When we look closer at the market, we can see that customers have been self-directing their IRAs for some time. A person who purchases a depository IRA and a mutual fund IRA may have three different IRAs, but the person has still directed the total IRA investment without the benefit of a consolidated account.

What, then, do we mean by a self-directed account? The key concepts commonly seem to include the following:

•Multiple investment options
•An ability for the customer to shift funds between investment
 alternatives
•A consolidated trust account

The menu may be limited to a few select choices or as broad as the choices of products advertised in the *Wall Street Journal*. The switches among investments may be limited in number or permitted totally at the customer's discretion. The trust account may provide comprehensive statements of account activity and value or more limited reporting. And fees can range from so high that they must be considered in the yield calculations, to so low the account itself could only be considered a loss leader. But to the extent the self-directed account demands investment choice--a choice that can include insurance products--and trust accounting, the product bridges financial cultures. The self-directed IRA is a product in which banking, insurance, and securities are certain to join.

The point, after all, is simple: Whoever gets the customer to establish the self-directed IRA is likely to capture the much-sought, long-term relationship. Why would a customer move if, through the consolidated self-directed account, adequate investment diversification can be obtained at a reasonable cost?

The self-directed account falls most comfortably into the broker's domain. What is more natural than for a broker to establish a single account in which the customer can trade stocks and bonds, buy investment company products, and hold government securities and municipals? Brokers sell annuities, and a list of CDs available from depository institutions around the country, with their varying terms and rates, can be examined for investment without leaving the broker's desk. Options can be purchased and a margin facility provided. Broker cash management accounts have consistently led banks in the consolidated report category. And with deregulation, brokers have managed to find ways to create, obtain, rent, or use, the trust facilities required.

Bankers are at more of a disadvantage than may initially be apparent. Attitudes form barriers as real as the institutional barriers found by law, regulation, and practice. Investment diversification demands risk, an element with which paternalistic bankers are uncomfortable, regardless of consumer demand. Investment alternatives to a properly trained banker spell disintermediation, which triggers the most basic fear that self-directed accounts virtually imply cannibalization of deposits.

What a difficult double-edged sword this particular interest rate decline has been. The reduced costs of funds has restored the profitability of many banks to historic levels while simultaneously putting at risk the security of those hotly contested, long-term deposits so critical to the liquidity needed for steady and profitable asset generation.

Nor have bank trust departments been noted for their imagination, yield, or state-of-the-art systems. Opening a large number of relatively small deposit accounts to active customer management is a prospect unlikely to warm the traditionally cool heart of the trust banker. But the conservative nature endemic to trust banking does have a purpose. In a historically strong bull market it should not require genius to increase a portfolio. But when interest rates rise, bonds and bond funds are certain to lose principal, and a Dow Jones index which can gain 100 points in a week can also lose 100 points in a week. Nor is market timing a reliable trait of even the most computerized professional investment portfolio manager.

Still, the trend toward self-direction, once begun, is unlikely to be reversed. Once more choices are available, it is hard to imagine the consumer wanting to return to the vanilla alternatives.

Admittedly, as young as the IRA market is, the self-directed IRA market is in its infancy. In 1986, we are only beginning to get adequate data to identify the profile of the self-directed customer, the specifics of market demand, and the required variations of investment mix and trust service. Yet given the size of IRA deposits and the competition from all major segments of the financial services industries--banks, brokerage houses, and insurance companies--few topics are likely to be more closely examined.

The purpose of this book is to bring together in one place reports from professionals attempting to understand and explain their positions

4

within the self-directed IRA marketplace. Granted, at this stage of our knowledge certain of the chapters may raise more questions than they answer, but overall, the works presented here are offered in the anticipation that they may at least serve as guides into this newly explored territory.

Market Research

To design successfully an IRA product for the self-directed customer, we must understand who that customer is and what that customer wants. The exercise, then, begins with market segmentation analysis and customer profile identification. Product design for the self-directed IRA begins with market research.

Here we have a somewhat unusual problem. Since 1982 the profile of the IRA customer has been fairly well-established. But the self-directed market segment is almost too new to permit more than preliminary views. Ironically, this particular configuration appeals perhaps most to the true marketer who always harbors a belief that past profiles do not begin to suggest the possibilities which will derive from the marketing effort itself.

The Raddon Financial Group opens this section with an excellent analysis of IRA market share, costs, and customer stability. This chapter's contribution is further enhanced by the analysis of the importance of mutual funds as an IRA investment option. A careful study of this piece should be helpful to any banker mapping a strategy to compete with brokers through positioning and promoting mutual fund IRAs.

Financial Services Group presents a succinct summary of the saver, searcher, and investor market segment analysis, which has distinguished the work produced by Market Facts, Inc., in this area. These investor segments have distinct profiles regarding fees, risk/return, investment preferences, and financial planning requirements. Failure to comprehend these distinctions and design products accordingly may dissatisfy savers and searchers, as well as investors.

The importance of Elizabeth Johnston-O'Connor's research is in the customer demographics of her market segmentation analysis. The discussion not only distinguishes the self-directed customer but also suggests the possibility of expanding IRA participation beyond the "wall" of those who have already contributed. With LIMRA being the premiere research organization for the life insurance industry, Dr. Johnston-O'Connor's chapter also provides valuable insights into the strategic planning going on among life carriers competing for self-directed IRA dollars.

1. The Importance of Mutual Funds to Self-Directed IRAs

OVERVIEW

The 1986 IRA season opened in a changing environment. As was predicted by the Raddon Financial Group in its August 1985 Client Update, self-directed IRAs are growing in importance. Market share for savings and loans and banks has dipped as competition for larger IRA accounts increased and as investors became more rate conscious. The savings and loan market share decreased to 23 percent in 1985 from 25.8 percent in 1984. The commercial bank market share fell from 28.2 percent in 1984 to 26.4 percent in 1985.

Yet total IRA deposits have skyrocketed. As of December 31, 1985, IRA deposits totalled $196.9 billion, up 41 percent from year-end 1984. The largest gains were in mutual fund IRAs and self-directed IRAs. IRA mutual fund deposits jumped 72 percent to $30.1 billion, to capture a 15.3% share of the IRA market. Self-directed IRAs, which may also include money invested in mutual funds, increased market share from 11.1 percent to 13.5 percent.

How can banks and savings and loans regain IRA shares? The answer is by adding mutual funds and self-directed IRAs to their product lines. Almost half of all major financial institutions already offer self-directed IRAs, usually through their discount brokerage operations. But only 17 percent provide a mutual fund choice for their clients' IRAs. This chapter will review Raddon research, demonstrate how mutual funds can increase your share of the IRA market, and take a look at self-directed IRA mutual fund offerings.

MARKET SHARE

The competition for IRAs has broadened as the individual IRA has grown in size. No longer is the battle simply among the financial

7

institutions. Brokerage firms, mutual funds, and life insurance companies have joined the fray.

At the same time, as substantial money accumulates in individual accounts, IRA holders have begun to look at a broader range of investment options. Raddon research showed that individuals begin to explore new investment options when the average amount invested in an IRA is $6,650.

Any individual who had invested the maximum amount allowed since 1982 would now have $8,000 in an IRA account. With the 1986 contribution, the amount will swell to $10,000 (or $20,000 per family if both spouses are employed). All these factors have combined to reduce the financial institutions' IRA share.

TABLE 1.1
Market Share by Industry
(in Dollar Holdings)

	1982	1984	1985
Commercial Banks	37.0%	28.2%	26.4%
Savings and Loans	21.0%	25.8%	23.0%
Mutual Funds	11.0%	12.5%	15.3%
Self-Directed IRAs	14.0%	11.1%	13.5%
Life Insurance	9.0%	9.5%	8.6%
Mutual Savings Banks	6.0%	7.0%	6.1%
Credit Unions	4.0%	5.9%	7.1%
Total Deposits	$32 billion	$140 billion	$196.9 billion

Market share data based on dollar holdings shows that financial institutions control approximately 55.5 percent of the IRA market, down from 61 percent in 1984. This drop in share has been caused by the continued growth of mutual funds and self-directed accounts. Mutual funds jumped from a 12.5 percent share to a 15.3 percent share, and self-directed IRAs increased from 11.1 percent to 13.5 percent.

Of financial institutions, only credit unions increased their share of the market, from 5.9 percent to 7.1 percent. Credit unions have recently been allowed to offer self-directed IRAs and Keoghs under certain restrictions set by the National Credit Union Administration.

IRA deposits held by investors differ significantly by financial institution sector. The typical savings and loan IRA holder has a larger amount on deposit than the typical bank customer. Raddon's Fall 1984 study showed median IRA deposits held by primary customers of savings institutions to equal $7,290. The primary commercial bank customer's median IRA balance was $6,260. Unless financial institutions can offer new IRA options, their market share will continue to erode.

How important is offering mutual funds and self-directed IRAs? Our Fall 1985 research showed that of those IRA holders with accounts at brokerage houses, mutual fund companies, and insurance companies, 13 percent rolled funds out of a bank or thrift to open the account. Over 20 percent of those with accounts at brokerage firms (self-directed IRAs) had rolled funds out of a bank or thrift.

These customers are likely to be the more affluent investors. About 26 percent of high income IRA holders have their accounts with a stock brokerage firm, and 21 percent use a mutual fund.

High income customers are also much more likely to open IRAs, about 4.7 times more likely than those earning less than $25,000. High income household usage had increased from 58 percent in the spring of 1984 to 70 percent in our Fall 1985 research study.

IRA COSTS

According to Functional Cost Analysis data, which fully allocates all costs over the account base, Table 1.2 lists estimated costs. The major components are account maintenance and interest posting.

TABLE 1.2

Assets	Commercial Banks	Savings Institutions
Up to $50 million	$37.42	$30.87
$50 to $200 million	35.86	28.36
Over $200 million	40.14	39.62

Source: *1984 Functional Cost Analysis*

Because competition for IRA funds is so fierce, the cost of funds is quite high. The cost is higher than small time deposits at many institutions and, in some cases, higher than jumbo costs. Spreads on this money are narrow or even negative because of the higher cost.

In a survey of savings institutions, less than 10 percent of respondents charged service fees, although each IRA costs between $30 and $35 annually to maintain. Only an average of $7 per IRA was spent on marketing, with 10 percent of advertising budgets allotted to IRAs.

The 1984 ABA Retail Deposit Services study showed that 6 percent of billion dollar commercial banks charge an IRA start-up fee and that 12 percent of this same group charge an annual maintenance fee.

TABLE 1.3

Banks	Small Time Funds Cost	IRA Funds Cost	Earnings	Spread on IRAs
< $50 million	10.297%	10.174%	10.516%	.342%
$50 to $200 million	10.228%	10.735%	10.640%	(.095)%
Over $200 million	10.320%	10.414%	10.595%	.181%
Savings Institutions				
< $50 million	9.825%	10.415%	10.573%	.158%
$50 to $200 million	10.473%	10.335%	10.356%	.021%
Over $200 million	10.702%	10.708%	10.238%	(.470)%

Source: *1984 Functional Cost Analysis*

Clearly the stability of IRA deposits determines the profitability of accounts. The one-time cost of attracting and opening an IRA can only be recouped through long term deposits. Since IRA balances are now reaching levels at which customers diversify for high yields, adding mutual funds and self-directed IRAs will increase IRA stability at the financial institution.

IRA STABILITY

Awareness that IRAs can be transferred has increased dramatically, an ominous finding for financial institutions. Our Fall 1984 study showed that one in four IRA holders was under the impression that once an IRA was opened it could not be transferred to another institution. By the fall of 1985 almost all investors were aware that IRAs could be transferred, although 57 percent indicated they would keep their IRA funds invested as they are now.

Another obstacle: Many IRA investors also view each year's contribution as a separate investment. The financial institution must compete each year to win the IRA contribution.

Rate Shoppers

Affluent investors (between the ages of 35 and 44 and with liquid assets between $5,000 and $10,000) were most likely to explore other IRA investment options. Over half indicated they would consider switching their IRA money.

IRA holders who consider switching begin their evaluations at an average balance level of $6,650. About 50 percent would begin considering new options with balances below $6,000. Only one in four would wait until his or her IRA reached $10,000 or more.

Financial Institution Image

The great majority of these IRA holders would consider their bank or savings association as a source for each and every investment. One-third would consider their bank or thrift for mutual funds, and 46 percent would do so for self-directed IRAs.

Unfortunately, the numbers change dramatically for those IRA holders who are using other sources for their IRAs. Of these individuals with IRAs at brokers, mutual funds, and insurance companies, over 40 percent said they would *not* be interested in purchasing any of these investments at banks or savings institutions.

This startling finding underscores the importance for financial institutions of offering alternative products before their IRA holders move to other sources. Once they transfer, it's very unlikely that the institution can win back these IRA deposits.

OFFERING THE MUTUAL FUND IRA

Mutual funds have emerged as one of the fastest-growing IRA investments, with a 15.3 percent share of a $196.9 billion IRA market. Mutual fund IRA share can be expected to continue to expand, since overall mutual fund popularity is at an all-time high.

In 1985 total mutual fund sales, including mutual funds in IRAs, are expected to reach $110.5 billion, compared with a previous record of $45.9 billion in 1984. Mutual funds hold 36 million accounts, representing 22 million households. Total assets of mutual funds in 1985 are now at a record $495 billion, up 34 percent from 1984's $370.68 billion. A rising stock market and investor interest in high yields are fueling these remarkable gains.

Financial institutions have a number of options in offering mutual funds for their IRAs, both by product and by investment company behind the product.

Types of Mutual Funds for IRAs

Mutual funds are portfolios of securities bought with money pooled from investors. Investors own a share or unit of the fund, which includes a percentage of each security while in the fund. The investor shares proportionately in the rise or fall of these securities in the fund and, consequently, in the profits or losses of the fund. The chief advantage is diversification of investments. Investors spread their risk by owning part of a large number of securities through the mutual fund.

Most investors automatically assume that mutual funds are open-end stock mutual funds. But the term "mutual funds" encompasses many other funds; some, such as money market funds, are similar to products that financial institutions are offering now without any regulatory concerns.

Mutual funds can consist of portfolios of stocks, government bonds, corporate bonds, or municipal (tax-free) bonds. Open-end funds are actively managed. Securities can be added or sold, depending upon management's assessment of the marketplace.

Financial institutions will want to provide a selection of mutual funds for their IRA customers.

GNMA Mutual Funds. These funds consist of mortgage-backed securities guaranteed by the Government National Mortgage Association. They provide the safety of government-guaranteed income and the high yields of mortgages (usually greater than CDs). They have become extremely popular as IRA investments.

Corporate Bond Mutual Funds. These funds provide high yields from corporate bonds. Various funds are available, ranging from conservative funds with high-grade bonds rated "A" or better, to high-yielding funds with "junk" bonds.

Municipal Bond Mutual Funds. IRAs should not be invested in these funds, since they produce tax-free income, which defeats the tax advantages of the IRA.

Common Stock Mutual Funds. There are almost as many common stock mutual funds as there are investors' goals. Each fund includes a statement of its investment strategy and goals prominently displayed on the prospectus. In general, there are four kinds of common stock mutual funds: growth funds, income funds, growth-income funds, and balanced funds.

Growth Funds. The primary investment objective is long term growth of capital. Management looks for capital gains from investments in companies it believes will grow quickly. The funds are risk-oriented and aggressive.

Income Funds. The primary investment objective is current income, usually from dividends. Management looks for larger companies that pay dependable dividends. These funds are considered conservative investments.

Growth-Income Funds. These funds aim for income and long term capital gains. In terms of risk, they are considered more conservative than growth funds, but more aggressive than income funds.

Balanced Funds. Management pursues an investment policy of "balancing" the portfolio. These funds are not exclusively common stock funds. They also include bonds and preferred stock of corporations.

In addition, there are many special purpose funds, including funds investing exclusively in gold mining companies, technology companies, foreign corporations, and national resource companies.

Why do IRA investors choose mutual funds? Perhaps the most important reason is high yields. About 53 percent of those using mutual funds in an IRA indicated they did so for a higher yield, according to Raddon research. At a time when CDs and money market funds are offering disappointing returns, mutual funds provide attractive yields.

Mutual funds can also offer investors a greater choice. Investors can choose from bonds, stocks, or government investments with all varieties of risk.

At the same time, mutual funds *do* pose a greater risk of loss of investment. Even with the safest type of mutual fund, the GNMA (Ginnie Mae) mutual fund, investors can lose part of their original investment when they sell. IRAs within CDs do not run this risk.

MUTUAL FUND INVESTMENT

The Raddon Financial Group's Spring 1985 research investigated current mutual fund investment among various market segments. While this research did not specifically target IRA holders, it provides a yardstick for mutual fund potential among the general population.

About 17 percent of all households currently own or have previously owned mutual funds. Predictably, high income households ($50,000 or more annual income) and high liquid asset households ($25,000 or more) had been mutual fund investors.

Financial institutions have an advantage in offering mutual funds to their customers, whether within an IRA or as an independent product. About 14.4 percent of all households would be very likely to purchase mutual funds through a financial institution. An even higher percentage of high income and high liquid asset investors would consider buying mutual funds through their financial institution, about 20 percent in each category.

Statistics on IRA holders reveal a strong opportunity for financial institutions. About one-third of those IRA holders considering other investments would buy a mutual fund IRA through their financial institution.

TABLE 1.4
Mutual Fund Usage

	% of All Households	% Who Currently Or Have Previously Owned Mutual Funds	Estimated Number of Households
Total	100%	17%	16.0 MM
Income			
Less than $25K	60%	8%	4.1 MM
$25K to $50K	20%	20%	3.4 MM
$50K plus	7%	45%	2.7 MM
Liquid Asset Holdings			
Less than $10K	64%	9%	4.9 MM
$10K to $25K	13%	24%	2.6 MM
$25K plus	13%	38%	4.2 MM
Age			
18 to 34	31%	9%	2.4 MM
35 to 44	19%	21%	3.4 MM
45 to 54	16%	25%	3.4 MM
55 to 64	15%	25%	3.2 MM
65 plus	19%	20%	3.2 MM

Source: *Raddon Financial Group Spring 1985 National Consumer Research*

START-UP OPTIONS

Until the Glass-Steagall Act is modified, banks will have limited options in mutual fund operations. The Securities and Exchange Commission has issued a new rule 3b(9), which requires banks to register a separate subsidiary for securities activities under certain conditions. This ruling also applies to offering mutual funds. Savings institutions and state banks may engage in mutual fund operations through independent subsidiaries.

Banks cannot generally organize, sponsor, or sell mutual funds under Glass-Steagall, but they have been allowed to act as a fund's investment advisor. Under a "no-load" 12(b)1 plan, they are also acting as "service agents."

TABLE 1.5

	% of All Households	% Extremely or Very Likely to Buy Mutual Funds through Their Bank or Thrift	Estimated Number of Households
Total	100%	14.4%	12.2 MM
Income			
Less than $25K	60%	14.0%	7.1 MM
$25K to $50K	20%	16.0%	2.7 MM
$50K plus	7%	20.0%	1.2 MM
Liquid Asset Holdings			
Less than $10K	64%	14.0%	7.6 MM
$10K to $25K	13%	12.0%	1.3 MM
$25K plus	13%	21.0%	2.3 MM
Age			
18 to 34	31%	14.0%	3.7 MM
35 to 44	19%	15.0%	2.4 MM
45 to 54	16%	12.0%	1.6 MM
55 to 64	15%	15.0%	1.9 MM
65 plus	19%	13.0%	2.1 MM

Source: *Raddon Financial Group Spring 1985 National Consumer Research*

Start-Up Choices for Financial Institutions

Manage a Mutual Fund. The institution can act as investment advisor and manager of a mutual fund under current law. The institution cannot, however, underwrite, organize, or sell the fund. Fees for the institution can range from 0.3 percent to 0.6 percent of the net assets of a mutual fund portfolio. An organizer, distributor, and marketing agent must be found for the fund. In choosing this method, the institution needs a strong investment advisory department and various registrations, including SEC, and the appropriate agency reviews (such as Comptroller approval).

Example: Security Pacific National Bank created its own family of no-load mutual funds, which includes a money market fund, a government securities money market fund, a high-yield bond fund, a California tax-exempt money market fund, and a California tax-exempt bond fund. Assets have grown to over $900 million. Dreyfus Corp., a mutual fund company, is acting as distributor, administrator, and marketer of the funds. Security

Pacific will inform its customers of the funds through the mail, telling them to contact Dreyfus for more information. Dreyfus will receive about 0.2 percent to 0.3 percent of the average net assets of the fund portfolios for its service.

Example: First Chicago markets mutual funds through their self-directed IRA. These funds include both 12b-1 funds managed by Dreyfus and funds that are managed by First Chicago.

Example: Chemical Bank manages five mutual funds with Fidelity Investments of Boston as a New York tax-exempt money market fund, an equity fund, an equity income fund, and a specialized portfolio fund.

Example: U. S. Trust Co. of New York manages a group of funds in a venture with Shearson Lehman Brothers.

Become a Service Agent for a Mutual Fund. Institutions provide shareholder and administrative services in return for about 25 to 30 basis points annually, based on the average daily net asset value of shares invested by the institution's customers. The mutual fund company markets the fund through a toll-free number, acts as manager, and underwrites the fund.

Underwrite Mutual Funds. Under current regulations, banks cannot underwrite mutual funds. If Glass-Steagall is modified to allow underwriting, mutual funds could become a substantial source of income to financial institutions. It could generate both asset management and portfolio commission revenues, as well as underwriting commissions in the case of load funds. In addition to a combined annual fee of 0.65 of average net assets under management for managing, distributing, and administering the funds, a sales charge of between 3.5 percent and 5 percent can be levied at the time customers purchase the funds. Generally, it is estimated that to break even the institution must accumulate about $100 million in assets invested in a mutual fund. Mutual fund companies claim they operate on a net margin of only 10 to 12 basis points (50-75 basis points gross margin).

Profits or losses will also be derived from holding the portfolio, whether stocks or bonds, until shares have been sold. If the stocks and bonds go up, your institution pockets the extra profit. If they go down before the shares are sold, your institution shoulders the loss.

Distribute a "Name Brand" Mutual Fund. Institutions are now distributing mutual funds through discount brokerage subsidiaries. Some institutions are also directly offering "name brand" mutual funds to IRA customers. In general, Glass-Steagall prohibits banks from distributing or selling any mutual funds.

Almost 75 percent of all mutual fund assets are now in no-load funds (including money market funds), and most investors prefer the no-load funds for obvious reasons. Yet institutions can only receive sales commissions if a sales fee is charged. Because of the proliferation of no-load funds, sales commissions have been squeezed. Currently, the institutions would receive about 2.5 percent of the sale as a sales commission. Under a 12b-1 (no-load) plan, the institution can act as a service agent for a fee.

Example: Fidelity, the nation's largest independent mutual fund company which manages $27.1 billion in assets, has launched its Partners in Profit program to wholesale its mutual funds to banks. Fidelity markets the product for the banks and pays them for access to their customers.

Example: Federated Investors, Inc., offers two IRA plans called "Banker's Choice" for banks to offer their customers. Funds include a stock trust, aggressive growth equity fund, and foreign securities fund. Banks receive a 25 basis point commission on deposits. Federated provides training and marketing support, such as a profile of the self-directed IRA customer, stats of ads, and a campaign theme. Banks pay for marketing the program.

CHOOSING THE MUTUAL FUND

Most institutions will probably decide to offer a "name brand" mutual fund, rather than start their own operation. This route will provide a way to acquaint the institution with the mutual fund business in order to

- Decide whether the institution has the expertise and capital to start its own mutual fund;
- Make a decision regarding the profitability of its own mutual fund compared to the resources needed to start the fund;
- Position itself to enter the market fully when and if regulations permit.

In deciding to affiliate with a mutual fund name, the financial institution should look for several features.

Reputation

The reputation of the fund and its recognition in the retail marketplace are the most important considerations. The majority of assets are concentrated in only about 20 companies. When you choose a mutual fund your customers know, half the job of selling is already done for you.

Marketing Support

Be sure the fund offers strong marketing support in the form of advertising, training, and free advice. In addition to providing your institution with advertising slicks and promotional brochures, investigate the

18

fund's own national advertising. Its brand name advertising promotes its name in the marketplace and directly affects your customers' recognition of the fund.

Performance

A significant proportion of your investors will select a fund based on its five-year performance. Choose a fund with a track record. Here are some factors that affect performance: rapid growth; overall size (the bigger the fund, the less the trading maneuverability, which may mean lower returns); change in portfolio managers (the manager responsible for a fund's strong performance may no longer be guiding the fund).

Fee Negotiation

The mutual fund company should be willing to negotiate fees with your institution, including load, retention, and sub-advisory fees.

Attitude

This intangible quality can become crucial as your institution ventures into the marketplace with mutual funds. Be sure the fund is willing to do everything it can to help your institution succeed. The fragile partnership between mutual funds and financial institutions has evolved quite recently, while rivalry has been a long-standing tradition. Make sure the mutual fund company has overcome that rivalry and truly wants your institution to succeed.

When considering a specific mutual fund company, ask these questions:

- •Will the mutual fund company be well known to your customers? How much advertising does it do within your area?
- •Is the mutual fund familiar with IRAs? Does it understand the regulations?
- •What are its mutual funds' track records? Consult *Money Magazine*, the *Wiesenberger Investment Co.* reports, and *Fortune*.
- •How will the mutual fund support your institution? Is ample marketing support available? Is the training program adequate?
- •Does the mutual fund company's current investor profile mirror your institution's customer profile? Will its products be attractive to your customers?
- •Is the mutual fund product line diversified? Can it offer your customers a choice? Does it offer a GNMA product? Is its stock growth fund competitive with other mutual funds?

•Do any of its products compete with your institution's product line (money market funds, etc.)? If so, can you resolve the problem?

•Can the mutual fund company absorb your business comfortably without back office problems? Or will your institution face complaints about service from its customers?

•Does the mutual fund's management philosophy complement your institution's outlook? (Remember, if the market turns against the mutual funds, your institution may be fielding the complaints.)

•Is the sales charge for the mutual funds high? Will sales suffer because of the large load?

•Will your institution be fairly compensated for its services? Does the mutual fund company seem willing to negotiate fees?

•Have all questions regarding conflicts of interest been answered to your satisfaction? Can your institution start its own fund or choose another mutual fund company after a reasonable period of time?

SELF-DIRECTED IRAS

Briefly defined, self-directed IRAs allow consumers to manage their own investments by choosing among a wide variety of brokerage-type products.

Research done by the Raddon Financial Group has shown that consumers have consistently expressed a strong interest in the self-directed IRA.

As previously noted, our Fall 1985 national research study showed that 46 percent of IRA holders who will be exploring new investment options for their IRAs would consider obtaining a self-directed account at their bank or savings association.

Self-directed accounts can be sold through brokerage subsidiaries with a full array of investment products, or they can be offered through non-registered institutions if the investments are limited to traditional bank and savings institution products and no-load 12b-1 mutual funds. As previously noted, financial institutions are acting as service agents for customers in making 12b-1 funds available and cannot offer investment advice.

If an institution creates its own self-directed IRA, it can use a money market deposit account as a holding tank for funds, thus retaining the ability to earn spread income on funds that would have moved elsewhere.

Other sources of income for self-directed accounts are set-up fees, annual maintenance fees, brokerage commissions, sharing of load fees from mutual funds, commissions from mutual funds, and 12b-1 service fees from mutual funds.

We will look at three programs that offer mutual funds through self-directed IRAs.

Federated

Federated offers two types of self-directed IRA plans, each with its own investment options and compensation plans.

Plan 1 provides the following types of investments:

- •A blue chip equity mutual fund
- •An income equity mutual fund
- •A growth/equity mutual fund
- •A high yield corporate bond fund

All funds are no-load funds. The financial institution receives 12b-1 compensation of 25 basis points of invested balances each year.

Plan 2 provides the following types of investments:

- •A blue chip equity fund
- •A high quality bond fund
- •A government fund composed primarily of GNMAs and FNMAs

All funds are no-load funds. With this plan the financial institution receives 25 basis points on yearly invested balances, as well as a 2 percent commission provided by Federated.

There is a back-end redemption fee of *2 percent* for the first seven years with this plan.

With both plans Federated provides statements to customers, all sub-accounting, and IRS reporting. A $10 fee per account per year is charged to the financial institution. This fee can be passed on to the customers in an annual maintenance fee. Institutions are charging $25 to $35 for these accounts.

Participating institutions can send a data tape that contains self-directed customers' other account information to Federated, and they will mail the customer a consolidated quarterly statement.

Example: Manufacturers Hanover offers a self-directed IRA that includes the Federated Stock Trust and the Federated Growth Trust, a blue chip and a growth fund.

Information on the mutual funds is provided through an 800 number staffed by licensed Federated employees. Because of the large volume of inquiries from Manufacturers Hanover's customers, Federated provides a special extension so that their sales agents are aware that they are dealing with Manufacturers Hanover customers.

The self-directed account also includes general brokerage service through Manufacturers Hanover's discount brokerage subsidiary.

Fidelity

Fidelity's self-directed account gives a financial institution's customers access to mutual funds, as well as general brokerage services.

The financial institution can use its own money market deposit account as a holding tank or use Fidelity's Money Market Mutual fund.

Fidelity's mutual funds include both load and no-load funds.

The Fidelity Magellan Fund carries a 3 percent front-end load charged to the customer. Their Equity Income Fund has a 2 percent front-end load. Fidelity's OTC and overseas funds will be added shortly.

Fidelity will share a portion of this income with the financial institution. There is no recurring income from these funds other than annual maintenance charges assessed by the financial institution.

Other Fidelity no-load funds are also available through its self-directed account. Compensation to the financial institution on these 12b-1 funds is 25 basis points.

Fidelity does the sub-accounting and statement mailings. The fee for this is approximately 35 cents per account per month.

Fidelity gives the institution the ability to provide a consolidated statement to customers using the financial institution's in-house software.

Example: Harris Bank of Chicago offers a self-directed IRA that includes three Fidelity mutual funds:

- The Daily Tax-Exempt Fund (no-load)
- The Magellan Fund (3 percent load)
- The Equity Income Fund (2 percent load)

In March 1986 Harris will make additional Fidelity funds available, including a no-load GNMA fund.

Harris charges a $25 annual maintenance fee and requires $1,000 to open the account. Other brokerage products are linked to the self-directed account through Harris' discount brokerage subsidiary.

Dreyfus

Dreyfus provides no-load 12b-1 funds as a part of self-directed IRA accounts. Financial institutions receive 25 to 30 basis points per year on invested balances. Dreyfus is also acting as administrator for mutual fund accounts that are managed by commercial banks.

Example: First National Bank of Chicago has a self-directed account through which the customer has access to general brokerage services, as well as four mutual funds:

- Dreyfus GNMA Fund
- Dreyfus General Aggressive Growth Fund
- Dreyfus General Money Market Fund
- First Lakeshore Diversified Asset Fund.

The three Dreyfus funds are 12b-1 funds, for which First Chicago receives 25 to 30 basis points of annual invested balances. The last fund is managed by First Chicago and administered by Dreyfus.

POSITIONING AND PROMOTION

Consider the following strategies to position your institution in the IRA marketplace and to promote mutual fund IRAs. These marketing ideas can boost your institution's image by adding mutual funds to your IRA line-up for greater market share and profitability.

Defensive Strategy

Many institutions have a justifiable fear of cannibalizing their own IRA CD deposits when offering mutual funds to IRA customers. One institution has overcome this concern by promoting both its CDs and its mutual funds in one ad. Only the rates on its CDs are listed. The investor must call to request its mutual fund yields.

Result: The institution will continue to sell its CDs without competition from its mutual fund yields. Yet those IRA investors who prefer mutual funds will be aware that this institution can accommodate them.

Building Continuity

Offer an expandable, "add-along" IRA option to the mutual fund and provide automatic transfers from a transaction account. Only about 41 percent of IRA holders deposit all their IRA money at once.

An expandable IRA can open up the IRA market to lower income taxpayers and provide convenience for higher income investors. It also adds stability to your IRA deposits by avoiding the idea that each year's deposit should be treated as a separate investment.

Mutual funds are particularly suited to the expandable IRA concept, because they have been sold for many years on the "averaging concept," in which an investor adds the same amount to a mutual fund every month, regardless of current yield or price.

The Procrastinator's IRA

Several institutions had strong successes with campaigns stressing convenience and last-minute IRA availability. Add mutual funds to this IRA product line-up.

Sample promotions: "The I've-got-10-minutes-that's-all IRA," newspaper ads with the IRA form included in the ad for the customer to complete and return, extended IRA lobby hours, mail-in IRA kits.

1986 is the second year in which investors must deposit IRA money by April 15. In previous years, IRA investors could postpone IRA deposits by filing a tax return extension.

Encouraging Rollovers/Transfers

Actively solicit rollovers and transfers from other IRA accounts, not just new deposits. Some investors will have sizeable accounts which include pension plan rollovers and other monies. Their IRA assets can far exceed the $10,000 maximum of most regular accounts.

Become the local expert on these rollovers with special promotions. Their substantial assets can offer your institution lucrative opportunities, compared to regular IRA holders.

CONCLUSION

Include mutual fund choices and a self-directed IRA in your IRA product line to increase your profitability and maintain market share. Consider the following reasons financial institutions need to offer the mutual fund IRA option:

Retaining Current IRAs. As IRA holders become more sophisticated and their investments reach balance levels between $6,000 and $7,000, they are likely to transfer IRAs to higher-yielding vehicles, such as mutual funds. Many of these investors would prefer to deal with their primary financial institution. But once these IRA holders transfer their funds, they are unlikely to consider returning their funds to a financial institution's IRA.

Attracting High Income Customers. High income customers are 4.7 times more likely to open IRAs, yet they also choose mutual funds and self-directed IRAs more often than do lower income customers. Use mutual funds and self-directed IRAs to attract these lucrative customers, and provide your financial institution with greater cross-selling opportunities.

Increasing Profitability Through IRA Stability. The one-time cost of opening an IRA is high. Unless financial institutions can retain that IRA, the cost will be greater than the gain. Mutual funds can provide an alternative by preventing customers from leaving your institution for higher-yield IRAs.

Mutual funds and self-directed IRAs are no longer esoteric options for your IRA holders. It's time to add them to your product line for greater profitability and a larger IRA market share.

2. Profiling the IRA Market: Savers, Searchers, and Investors

In today's financial marketplace, there are basically three types of "shoppers": Savers, Searchers, and Investors.

Savers are found primarily in mature households whose objectives are to maximize their returns on conservative investments. They are characteristically price-sensitive, bank-oriented, and have little need for financial advice.

By contrast, because they are typically busy people, Searchers strongly feel the need for guidance regarding investment and financial management. Full-service firms and "one-stop" financial service sources are ideal for this segment.

Investors, on the other hand, actively manage their own funds and are willing to take on more risky investments, such as stocks and bonds. Investors favor brokerage firms and mutual fund companies over banks to service their financial needs.

While it's true that Investors are slightly more affluent than Savers and Searchers, income is not as important a factor as you might think. In fact, one of the key discriminating factors in determining behavior is *attitude*.

A perfect example of attitude is illustrated by how people use cameras. If you did a cluster analysis of camera usage, you'd find there are some people who never use a camera, or have one, but never take it out of the drawer. Then there are those who only take pictures on special occasions, like birthdays, weddings, graduations, and so on. Finally, there are those who feel photography is an art. They're the ones with very complicated cameras and lenses, concerned with lighting, F-stops, etc. Yet the fact that some people don't fiddle with cameras and would rather buy someone else's pictures is merely an attitude. The way people view income is different: There are those who don't want to be involved in their own investing; it could be due to the lack of time or interest, or it could be because of a lack of money.

Aside from attitude, surely we're all familiar with such stories as the one where a mailman generated $14,000 in brokerage commissions in one year, or the one about the little old lady who drew only Social Security as income, but had a $10,000 savings account balance. These examples illustrate that the Investors do not necessarily represent the affluent segment.

TABLE 2.1
Market Segmentation

Savers

• Conservative
• Price-Sensitive
• Bank-Oriented
• Little Need for Financial Advice

Searchers

• Busy Lifestyles
• Need Financial Guidance
• Favor Full-Service Firms

Investors

• Risk-Takers
• Actively Participate in Financial Management
• Favor Brokerage Firms, Mutual Fund Companies

The reason great care has been taken to segment the market into Savers, Searchers and Investors is that we've found that financial activity is quite easy to explain in most cases using these categorizations. For example, *IRAs are most likely held by Savers*. Further, we've found that *three out of every four households that have SDAs are Investors*.

IRAs

Institutions

In order to meet the preferences of Savers, banks and thrifts continue to dominate the IRA market. Almost two-thirds of all households with IRAs have contributions in a bank or thrift; one-half of all IRA assets are in a commercial bank, savings and loan, or savings bank. Insurance companies, full-service brokers, and mutual fund companies each manage an additional 11 to 14 percent of all IRA dollars.

Convenience, safety, and rates of return are the primary factors guiding consumers in selecting institutions for their IRAs. Sixty-one percent of all households selected their institution in part because they already had other accounts there. Further, more than two-fifths deposited their 1984 contribution where previous contributions had been made. Government insurance of funds, which will be discussed in more detail later, was important to more than two-fifths of all households when they selected their institutions. Finally, one-third looked, in part, for the highest rates available.

With an overriding motivation being convenience, then, it should be no surprise to learn that 87 percent of all households used the same institution for their 1984 IRA contribution as in 1983. In fact, only 30 percent of all households "shopped around" for institutions in 1984. Seven out of every 10 households with IRAs did not even bother to explore other options in the IRA market.

Why? It seems that most consumers (69 percent) are satisfied with their current accounts. Further, those that have switched institutions have done so primarily in search of greater returns.

This is very good news for institutions offering IRAs, especially banks and thrifts, because once you acquire an IRA client, you will most likely retain that client.

FIGURE 2.1
Distribution of Total IRA Assets by Institution
September 1985

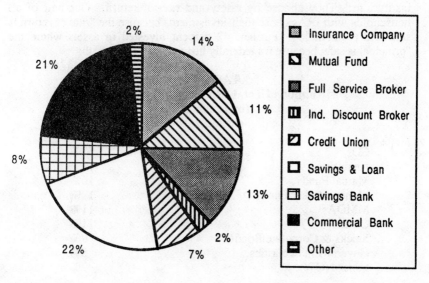

- Insurance Company
- Mutual Fund
- Full Service Broker
- Ind. Discount Broker
- Credit Union
- Savings & Loan
- Savings Bank
- Commercial Bank
- Other

TABLE 2.2
Distribution of Total IRA Accounts by Institution
(by Household)
September 1985

Commercial Bank	13%
Savings & Loan	23%
Insurance Company	18%
Full-Service Broker	13%
Mutual Fund Company	13%
Credit Union	11%
Savings Bank	9%
Other	4%
Independent Discount Broker	3%

Investments

IRA owners, reflecting their Saver-like financial attitudes, prefer not to take on much risk in their retirement investing; almost one-half choose to "play it conservatively." Therefore, it's no shock to see that 50 percent of all households with IRAs have some contributions in CDs. In fact, 46 percent of all IRA dollars are held in CDs. Annuities and mutual funds are also common investments, accounting for 13 percent and 11 percent of all IRA assets, respectively.

Consumers select IRA investments in the same way they select institutions: They choose by safety and rate of return. One-half of all households with IRAs chose their investments because the "rate of return is safe and predictable." Further, 42 percent invested in assets where the "principal is safe, because it's federally insured."

TABLE 2.3
Distribution of Total IRA Accounts by Investment
(by Household)
September 1985

CDs	50%
Annuities	19%
Mutual Funds	16%
Money Market Funds	12%
MMDAs	11%
Other	11%
Stocks & Corporate Bonds	9%
Government Securities	5%
Super-NOW	2%

Moreover, we find that most consumers invested in the same vehicles in 1984 as they did in 1983, more than eight out of ten, to be specific. They did so because they're satisfied with their current investments (69 percent), and the major source of dissatisfaction was poor return. More than 60 percent of those who have switched investments were looking for a higher rate of return.

Fee-Sensitivity

As stated earlier, Savers are price-sensitive. This, too, is reflected in their IRA activity. The vast majority of these households feel it's very important to have an account with a low maintenance fee. However, it is not at all their foremost concern in the selection process.

Currently, although fees range widely, IRA owners most often pay between $11 and $25 to open an account, between $6 and $25 for account maintenance, and $5 or less to switch or terminate investments, if they pay a fee at all. Yet their price sensitivity reveals these households' Saver-oriented values. If their current fees were to rise by $10, four out of ten would still keep the account, and only one out of 10 would definitely close the account. However, when faced with a $25 fee increase, only one out of ten households would not take its IRA to another institution; five out of 10 would go elsewhere.

Not surprisingly, the older a consumer is and the greater his or her household income, the less price-sensitive he or she is.

FIGURE 2.2
Distribution of Total IRA Assets by Investment
September 1985

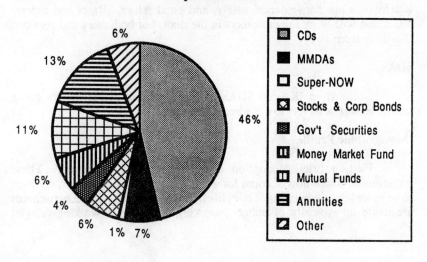

Rate-Sensitivity

IRA owners appear to be even more rate-sensitive than fee-sensitive. In fact, when selecting their most recent IRAs, 35 percent of all owners named rate of return as their foremost concern. Most owners feel it's very important to have the highest annual return possible for their IRAs.

Regarding fees, we've observed that dissatisfaction with rates of return will prompt a consumer to switch to other investments or institutions. Therefore, IRA owners are sensitive to both rates and fees. While rates play a more important role in the selection process, dissatisfaction in either area will cause a customer to switch.

Further, small fee increases do not seem to drive many current customers away. It is advisable when an institution offers an IRA to do a little cost-benefit analysis to see if a small fee increase would more than pay its way, assuming a 10 percent customer attrition rate.

Federal Insurance

Finally, the importance IRA owners place on FDIC or FSLIC insurance should be reemphasized. Seventy-one percent of these households rate federal insurance as a very important factor in the IRA selection process. And, to reiterate previous findings, federal insurance is a priority for both institution selection and investment selection. This is to be expected, in light of the Saver's desire for safe, conservative investments.

Now we all have a good idea of the typical IRA owner. His or her values as a Saver dictate priorities with respect to institutions, investments, fees, rates of return, and federal insurance. The average household most often has its IRA in a bank or thrift, with the funds invested in CDs. The watchwords are convenience, safety, and good return. Rates and federal protection will bring the customers in the door, but both rates and fees can also drive them away.

SDAs

Going from IRAs to SDAs is like switching gears: We're going from a market of Savers to a market of Investors.

Demographic Profile

First, a brief description of self-directed IRA owners: These households, which now account for 16 percent of all IRA owners, do seem to be more upscale in terms of both lifestyle and finances. These households are made up typically of either a working couple or a working (single) individual. Household size is small, usually one or two people. Heads of households tend to be between the ages of 40 and 59, with the average age at 47.

Financially these households are significantly wealthier than the average U.S. family. Most have an annual income exceeding $30,000 (and the average for this group is $41,000), compared to the national average of $24,000. They hold primarily professional and managerial positions, and the majority have had at least some college; more than one-half have a college degree.

At this point, it is judicious to step back and take a look at this profile. If these statistics had been presented without the common denominator--households with self-directed IRAs--whom would they describe? Investors, rather than Savers or Searchers? High income and net worth, well-educated professionals? To some, it would sound like the typical full-service brokerage client.

If more evidence is needed, there's a much higher incidence of stock and bond ownership among self-directed IRA owners than among all U.S. households: 69 percent, compared to 24 percent. Further, 44 percent of those with SDAs selected a full-service brokerage firm for their IRA contributions, while only 13 percent of regular IRA owners have placed their contributions with full-service brokers.

TABLE 2.4
Distribution of Total IRA Accounts by Type of Account
by Institution
(by Household)
September 1985

	All IRAs	Self-Directed IRAs
Commercial Bank	31%	17%
Savings & Loan	23%	13%
Insurance Company	18%	11%
Full-Service Broker	13%	44%
Mutual Fund Company	13%	25%
Credit Union	11%	6%
Savings Bank	9%	10%
Other	4%	7%
Independent Discount Broker	3%	8%
Discount Broker at Bank	**	3%

**Less than .5%

TABLE 2.5
**Distribution of Total IRA Assets
by Type of Account by Institution**
(by Household)
September 1985

	All IRAs	Self-Directed IRAs
Savings & Loan	22%	11%
Commercial Bank	21%	12%
Insurance Company	14%	5%
Full-Service Broker	13%	39%
Mutual Fund Company	11%	13%
Savings Bank	8%	7%
Credit Union	7%	4%
Independent Discount Broker	2%	4%
Other	2%	5%

Therefore, the obvious question at this juncture is: Are self-directed IRAs being bought or sold? In other words, are they just being bought by current customers of the institutions offering them, or are they being aggressively sold by these institutions to new as well as existing clients? This point is critical to the future demand of this product and will be dealt with later in this chapter.

Psychographic Profile

As stated before, the group just described accounts for 16 percent of all IRA owners today. Yet the potential demand for self-directed IRAs is much larger. Currently, 6 percent of IRA owners are interested in opening a self-directed IRA, and 6 percent of IRA prospects have indicated such an interest.

As these accounts become more tailored to the needs of the Investor segment, especially with regard to flexibility, risk, convenience, and the availability of financial planning, the demand for such products will escalate. Each of these critical motivational factors must be examined more closely.

Flexibility. Many households are attracted to the self-directed IRA because of its inherent flexibility. Indeed, they look for flexibility in both the institution and in the investments. Roughly one-third of all households with self-directed IRAs select institutions and investments based on the flexibility of the self-directed IRA investment structure. In fact, 41 percent of all SDA owners have switched investments.

Thus, institutions providing the greatest range of investments and the easiest transfer of self-directed IRA funds from one investment to another will experience the greatest growth in demand.

Risk and Return. This is the second factor motivating the self-directed IRA owners. As is characteristic of the Investor segment, this group is out to get the best return they can. Many of these households have invested their contributions in stocks, corporate bonds, and mutual funds to achieve the greatest return possible, a fact which makes them two to three times as likely to invest in these assets as IRA owners in general. Fully one-fifth of these households have invested their contributions in non-traditional products, such as precious metals and zero coupon bonds, in order to secure above-average returns. And a significant portion of self-directed IRA owners describe their investment strategy for retirement planning as *aggressive*.

TABLE 2.6
**Distribution of Total IRA Accounts
by Type of Account by Investment**
(by Household)
September 1985

	All IRAs	Self-Directed IRAs
CDs	50%	34%
Annuities	19%	9%
Mutual Funds	16%	36%
Money Market Funds	12%	22%
MMDAs	11%	7%
Other	11%	20%
Stocks & Corporate Bonds	9%	33%
Government Securities	5%	14%
Super-NOW	2%	1%

Thus, as typical Investors the self-directed IRA customers want to take on additional risk in their retirement investing, as they have in other aspects of their investment activity. A self-directed IRA structure catering to this need is strongly desired by this segment.

Convenience. While the self-directed IRA owner is not usually motivated by convenience in everyday financial activity, this does not appear to be the case for the self-directed IRAs themselves.

34

TABLE 2.7
**Distribution of Total IRA Assets
by Type of Account by Investment**
(by Household)
September 1985

	All IRAs	Self-Directed IRAs
CDs	45%	24%
Annuities	13%	4%
Mutual Funds	11%	14%
Money Market Funds	6%	20%
MMDAs	7%	4%
Other	6%	10%
Stocks & Corporate Bonds	6%	19%
Government Securities	4%	13%
Super-NOW	1%	**

**Less than .5%

Indeed, as with regular IRA owners, these households cite convenience as a primary consideration in selection of institutions; 52 percent made their choice in part because they already had other types of accounts there. In addition, when making their decision SDA households also consider factors such as where their previous contributions have been made, the convenience of location, and banking hours.

Therefore, these households are attracted by the convenience features of self-directed IRAs, a fact which enhances the opportunities to cross-sell from other financial products to self-directed IRAs.

Financial Planning. The fourth key factor for these households is the availability of financial planning advice.

This group feels that financial planning is very important. Further, they place a high priority on planning for retirement, even though it's almost two decades away for most of these households. Yet they are quite financially sophisticated in their own right. Therefore, while they value the financial advice of professionals, these households feel it is crucial to have personal control over their investment decisions.

However, there is a key secondary group here, a significant minority (25 percent) that is more reliant on financial advice. Their contribution strategy is guided by the recommendations of a trusted advisor. Further, almost half of all self-directed IRA owners choose their institutions because of the availability of good investment counseling.

Therefore, most households choose self-directed IRAs so they may actively participate in the management of their retirement funds. This motivation is completely in step with the Investor's psychographic profile. However, an institution offering financial planning services along with their self-directed IRAs will appeal to a smaller, yet still significant secondary group of self-directed owners.

In summary, the self-directed IRA owner is generally an active investor, upscale, and financially sophisticated. This household is typified by many Investor-type motivations such as taking on greater risk to get a better return, needing greater flexibility in their investment portfolio, and actively managing their own funds. Unlike the typical Investor, however, these households appreciate the convenience features of these accounts and occasionally desire investment guidance. Institutions which incorporate these features into their self-directed IRA structure will prosper from the growth in self-directed IRA demand.

POTENTIAL

It must be emphasized, however, that the self-directed IRA market is still fairly new, so these statistics should be reviewed in this light. The profile describes those to whom self-directed IRAs have been sold, not necessarily those who are interested in buying. For example, who would ever think of marketing self-directed IRAs to steel workers on the south side of Chicago? Yet in one study we found one south side bank with $17 million in self-directed IRAs from a total of just 19 people. It seems that as the steel industry began to have problems, the south side steel mill closed down, and some workers that had been at the mills for twenty and thirty years were pensioned out at $600,000 to $700,000.

At its young age, the self-directed IRA, appears to be *bought* by current clients, rather than *sold* to new and existing clients, at least to some extent.. The demographics support this. Given the demographic and psychographic profile of current self-directed IRA owners, it is critical to package this product effectively and market it aggressively to achieve the greatest potential growth in demand.

Now it is important to look at the key issues regarding SDA pricing and promotion.

PRICING SDAs

While most SDA owners reported paying no fees for opening, switching, or terminating their accounts, six out of ten households were charged an annual maintenance fee, usually between $11 and $25 (26 percent). Another 15 percent of these households pay $26 to $50 annually.

Surprisingly, though, this segment is fee-sensitive, while not as sensitive as that of IRA owners in general. A $10 fee increase would cause

50 percent of all SDA owners to *think* about going elsewhere, but the remaining 50 percent would remain loyal. Meanwhile, a $25 fee increase would only retain about 20 percent of current owners; 40 percent of the owners would definitely go elsewhere.

Finally, considering the importance this segment places on switching investments within their self-directed IRAs, *the path of least resistance for institutions in search of additional fee revenue is in the area of switching.*

PROMOTING SDAs

Promotion effectiveness must be analyzed. Current SDA owners report that the best way to tell them about a new financial product is via direct market and print advertising. Specifically, 59 percent of these households identified brochures as effective promotion vehicles, and 45 percent said a letter worked well. Further, *39 percent of all SDA owners have either initiated or added to an investment as a result of having received some type of promotional mailing.*

Print advertising, especially in the local newspaper or in financial magazines, was also cited as an effective means of promotion by about 40 percent of this segment. In fact, *27 percent of all SDA owners have either initiated or added to an investment due to a newspaper or magazine ad.*

What does this segment read, then? More than nine out of ten read the local paper regularly, and three out of ten SDA households read the *Wall Street Journal.* The most widely-read financial magazine among these households is *Money* (17 percent), followed by *Business Week* (11 percent), and *Fortune* (7 percent).

3. The Impact of IRAs: An Insurance Industry Perspective

Since IRAs became widely available in 1982, they have had a significant impact on what Americans do with their savings dollars. To provide a backdrop for trends in self-directed IRAs, this chapter primarily looks at the IRA market as a whole. Specifically, we will explore

- How big the pie is, and how big it is likely to get in the near future
- Who is investing in IRAs, why, when, and what they want
- Where market rates were after the 1982 tax year and now
- What insurance companies are doing, particularly with self-directed accounts (SDAs)
- What the marketer can do to secure more of the market

The IRA market blossomed from about $5 billion in 1981 to $28 billion for the 1982 tax year (January 1, 1982, to April 15, 1983). With totals increasing by approximately $3 billion per year ever since, 1985 is expected to top the $35 billion mark.

The Life Insurance Marketing and Research Association (LIMRA) estimates that the total dollars in IRAs as of year-end 1985 was over $200 billion. That is more than the *total combined assets* of the three largest diversified financial companies: FNMA (Fannie Mae), American Express, Aetna Casualty; or the largest commercial bank, Citicorp; or the three largest life insurers; The Prudential Insurance Company of America, Metropolitan Insurance Companies, and Equitable Life Assurance of America. In the future, with a steady economy, the maturing of the "baby boomers" (the large number of people born in the 15 years after World War II), and relatively unchanged legislative action toward IRAs, we can expect the annual investment in IRAs to continue to increase.

INVESTORS' MOTIVATION

On the whole, IRA investors want to protect their financial security for retirement, but they especially want to avoid Uncle Sam's taking more of their income than necessary, as demonstrated in Table 3.1.

TABLE 3.1

The Most Important Reasons for Contributing to an IRA[1]

	Percent of IRA Owners Indicating "Very Important"
To deduct IRA contributions from taxes	87%
To save for retirement	67%
To defer taxes on interest	58%
To ease concerns about social security	46%

These results are taken from a comprehensive study of the expanded IRA market conducted at LIMRA in April 1983. The survey was sent to a panel of 5,000 households demographically balanced to reflect United States households. Seventy-six percent of the surveys were returned. More recent studies of the market have generally replicated the findings of this study. Any exceptions to that will be indicated.

Among those respondents who did not contribute to an IRA, the most common reason was a lack of extra funds to lock away.

MARKET SEGMENTATION

How can we tell who can and who cannot invest in IRAs? Not surprisingly, income is the best predictor: The greater the income, the greater the likelihood of investing. Sixty percent of those households with incomes over $50,000 (in 1981 dollars) invest in IRAs. With each lower income category, there is a steady decline in the percentage of households investing in IRAs, to a low of only five percent of those households with incomes under $10,000 who invest in IRAs.

Rather than look at each demographic characteristic one at a time, it may be more profitable to look at customer profiles to get a better idea of who these people are and how they may match your markets. To do this we took all of the household demographics that we measured in our study in June 1984: age, income, occupation, education, life stage, geographic region, household size, marital status, and type of family or non-family, and analyzed them using a sequential analysis of variance. This technique helps

FIGURE 3.1 Segmenting the IRA Market*

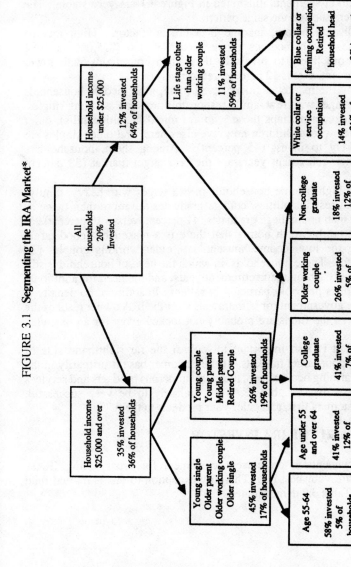

Good target markets →

Poor target markets

Data collected June 1984. Age, education, and occupation reported for household head only.

determine demographics which are most important for predicting buying behavior and help provide a sense of who the people are, not just what categories they fit.

The market segments illustrated in Figure 3.1 are very stable. The 1982 IRA owners showed the same pattern.

As indicated before, income is a crucial factor. High income households--those with incomes above about $30,000 ($25,000 in 1981 dollars)--are more likely to invest in IRAs than households with lower incomes (35 percent, versus 12 percent, respectively).

Refining the market segments even more, high income households that are in life stages with few family responsibilities such as young singles, older parents (except perhaps those who are mired in tuition bills), older working couples whose children now live elsewhere, and older singles are even more likely to invest (45 percent). Among them, householders approaching their retirement years are the best target market (58 percent invested).

Among high income households in life stages with heavy, family-related financial responsibilities, college graduates are more than twice as likely to invest than non-college graduates (41 percent, versus 18 percent).

It is certainly worth noting that there is a reasonably good target market among the low income households: older working couples (26 percent invested). These households, in which the head of household is still working, are approaching their retirement years, and the need for additional retirement funds is probably particularly salient. In addition, no penalty is imposed by the government for withdrawals after the IRA owner reaches the age of 59-1/2, so the funds are probably not locked away for an extended period.

Finally, it is also important to look at the far right-hand side of Figure 3.1, the poor target markets. If the customer base is primarily in the blue collar or farming occupations, there are numerous products and services geared for these markets, but IRAs are unlikely to be very successful. Know your customers first, and tailor your products to them.

HOW TO REACH THE IRA INVESTOR

Why concentrate on current customers for cross-selling IRAs? Because they are your best bet. The only exception to this is mutual fund companies, as Table 3.2 demonstrates.

TABLE 3.2
IRAs Established by Previous Customers[2]

	Percent Repeat Customers
Credit Unions	97%
Commercial Banks	86%
Thrifts	81%
Stockbrokerage Firms	78%
Insurance Companies	72%
Mutual Fund Companies	45%

Choosing the best potential customers--those that match the good target markets--can be accomplished with the use of a good customer information file. Such a file should have as much relevant information about a customer as possible. For instance, how many of your products does that customer have, and what demographic information, such as age, income, and life stage, is available?

It may seem like an awesome task, but it is likely that much of the important information can be found on the customer applications that you already have on file. The extent to which your company is doing financial planning with your customers will determine how extensive your customer files can be. You can also survey your current customers to get the necessary information. An anonymous survey would provide some of the more sensitive information, such as income, but it would be restricted to descriptions of your customer base as a whole. For many thrifts or specialized institutions this may be sufficient; for those who need more detailed information about individual customers, confidentiality of the data would be a critical concern.

The investment of time and effort involved in getting such a file up and running will start showing a return when you find you have saved on development costs of products that may not fit your primary market, not to mention the improved return from a mail or telephone campaign directed at a refined target population of customers.

When considering ad campaigns, where do you place your advertisements? You know whom you are targeting, so try to reach them through their places of work, direct mail, or newspaper ads, as Table 3.3 shows.

It will come as no surprise that January to April 15th is by far the biggest IRA investment season, so position your ads to capture the new money coming in.

TABLE 3.3
Advertising Sources Recalled and Considered Best by IRA Investors[3]

	Recalled	Considered Best*	Considered Best Among Those Recalled
Newspaper Ad	86%	15%	17%
TV Commercial	75%	5%	7%
Direct Mail	67%	19%	28%
Radio Commercial	54%	1%	2%
Magazine Ad	43%	--	--
Information at Work	35%	15%	43%
Billboard	19%	--	--

*Respondents had the opportunity to rate other non-advertisement media among media sources considered best. Therefore, this does not add to 100 percent.

DESIRABLE VEHICLE CHARACTERISTICS

Investors say that they are most concerned with high return, followed closely by high security. Of the remaining characteristics evaluated in LIMRA's 1983 study, their order of importance from highest to lowest were no fees, guaranteed life income, flexibility, service, disability waiver, and convenience. Closer examination of these characteristics suggests two that may be somewhat misrepresented by the data.

The first is flexibility. As IRAs start building into respectable sums of money, the need for diversification is likely to become more apparent. Self-directed accounts (SDAs) can provide just the flexibility required. By offering one account with multiple vehicles (such as a family of mutual funds among which investors can switch), and/or stocks, face amount certificates (such as CDs), and limited partnerships, the investor can diversify, minimize paperwork, and get one statement of IRA holdings from one source.

The second characteristic that may be underestimated by our respondents is convenience. Although people like to think their choice and the management of their funds is very active, discriminating, and purposeful, convenience may play a much larger role than most of us would like to admit. The implication is that you should make it easy to invest in your product by providing payroll deduction, direct mail, or telemarketing, with specialists who can do the paper work.

A good example is a thrift in the Hartford area, Northeast Savings, which is currently running a television ad campaign that promotes an IRA kit. If you call the 800 number supplied, it will send you a kit that enables you to open an IRA "in the comfort of your own home. Just send the completed forms with a check, or make some alternative arrangement, such as a loan, to open your account."

It might be wise to make it uncomfortable for a customer to get out of an investment by adding back-end loading (closeout fees). Such an arrangement could help prevent "runs" on your accounts for insignificant changes in interest rates. Some prospective customers may be hesitant to lock their funds into a company without some guarantee that the return will be competitive. That, too, can be designed into your product, much like the one offered by Union Central, an insurance company based in Ohio. It not only provides competitive, current rates for its annuity products, but also agrees to waive or significantly decrease the closeout fee should their product not remain competitive with treasury bill rates.

MARKET SHARES

Product design is of much greater concern now than it was in the 1982 tax year when CDs were offering very high rates. For that year CDs captured 39 percent of the market, making them by far the most popular choice. As investors experience rate shock from the lower rates now available, changes in market share reflect their concern. For instance, SDAs, which only had 6 percent of the market in 1982, may be as high as 16 percent for the 1985 tax year. The changes since the 1982 tax year can be seen in each institution's market share. The growth in self-directed accounts is most likely to be reflected in the increased market share of the mutual fund companies and stockbrokerage houses, as shown in Figure 3.2.

FIGURE 3.2
IRA Market Share Trends[4]

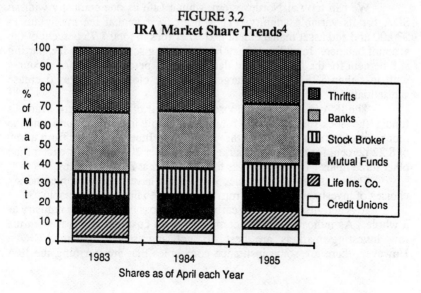

INSURANCE COMPANY IRAs

SDAs are also offered through insurance companies. A survey of insurance companies conducted by LIMRA in September 1985 shows that a number of insurance companies, especially the big ones (Prudential, Northwestern Mutual, John Hancock, New York Life, etc.) offer self-directed accounts for IRAs. In most cases the SDAs are offered for annuities. Although there are a variety of types of annuities, they all share the concept of guaranteed lifetime payout, which can only be offered through an insurance company. There can also be various investment alternatives for annuities, including the most common self-directed account: a family of mutual funds among which investors can switch. Less common are limited partnerships, zero coupon bonds, and stocks and bonds.

Regarding different types of fees:

•Start-up fees are not charged by most companies
•Modest maintenance fees ($15.00 to $40.00 a year) are common
•Vehicle change fees were charged less often
•Closeout fees (often on a sliding scale) were charged more often than not. These charges help ensure that the company will make some profit on the customer's account.

One company reported that it has offered a self-directed account since the inception of IRAs in the late 1970s, but most companies surveyed initiated their self-directed accounts in 1982 through 1985. It is likely that many more insurance companies will be developing self-directed accounts in the near future.[5]

We can look at Northwestern Mutual Life as one company with an SDA for its variable annuity. They limit their annual fee maximum to $30.00 and add asset management and other fees to total 1.75 percent of the account balance. In addition, they have a sliding scale closeout fee starting at 8 percent for the first year and declining by 1 percent a year for accounts with less than $25,000. For larger sums, the closeout charges decrease substantially.

The IRA investor can choose among four of Northwestern Mutual's funds: the stock fund, the bond fund, the multiple investment fund, and the money market fund. Rates for the year ending June 1985 went from a low of 8.22 percent for the money market fund to over 20 percent for each of the other three funds. The highest was the bond fund at 26.22 percent.[6]

Other insurance companies with SDAs have between three and six choices of investment vehicles, from bond funds to limited partnerships.

IRA activity is still in its early stages across the insurance industry as a whole. As indicated earlier, companies with customers primarily in the low investing markets are best off not aggressively pursuing IRAs. However, there are some insurance companies that are pursuing the IRA market and doing well with SDAs that are combined with annuities or other attractive products. As investors' balances increase and as their concerns about lifetime income become more salient, insurance companies may do very well in this market.

CONCLUSION

There are vast opportunities in the IRA market, a market that is big and getting bigger. More than half of those with high incomes, particularly those with fewer family-related financial responsibilities who are approaching their retirement years, are likely to invest in IRAs. In contrast, less than 10 percent of those householders with incomes under about $30,000, those who are not older working couples, and those who are in blue collar or farming occupations invest in IRAs.

Before deciding to pursue IRA investors aggressively, be sure your customers (your best target market), are also among the reasonably good IRA target markets. A good customer file with demographic information such as age, income, and life stage can be an enormous help in pinpointing your target markets. Promoting IRA investments starting at less than $2,000 may also attract potential investors who are unaware that there is no minimum amount. Once a customer chooses one company with which to place his or her IRA, that company can at least be assured that it will be used as a comparison against competitors.

Once a decision has been made to pursue the IRA market, consider using newspaper and direct mail advertising, especially from December through April, the peak investing season. Consider providing a payroll deduction arrangement with companies with which you have already arranged payroll deduction or direct payroll deposit arrangements. Make it easy for the customer to invest with you and easy to stay with you. Offer SDAs for multiple investment options, especially now that CDs are less attractive. Perhaps include a closeout fee in the early years, especially if you guarantee competitive rates. Then watch the number of your IRAs grow!

NOTES

[1]E.J. Johnston-O'Connor, *IRA Sweepstakes*, Life Insurance Marketing and Research Association, Hartford, Conn., 1984, p. 10.
[2] Ibid, p. 14.
[3] Ibid, p. 22.
[4]*IRA Reporter,* Protean Financial Corporation, Cleveland, OH, June 28, 1985, p. 4.
[5]*Some IRA Questions,* Products and Services News and Trends, Life Insurance Marketing and Research Association, Hartford, Conn., December 1985.
[6]*IRA Reporter*, August 23, 1985, pp.5-8.

Regulatory Issues

Banks and thrifts have been excluded from many aspects of the securities business by legislation and regulation. The self-directed account, however, will demand that the depository institution manufacture or otherwise obtain a facility for securities transactions within the IRA.

In addition to providing an excellent overview of IRA regulations, attorney David Shelton examines the types of self-directed IRAs which may be offered by insurance companies, securities firms, and depository institutions. In the process, he focuses upon the implications of several important topics, such as bank discount brokers, member bank common trust funds, and the 1986 SEC Rule 3b-9. The discussion suggests throughout the possibilities of joint ventures between various segments of the differently constrained segments of the financial services industries.

4. Self-Directed IRAs: Legal and Regulatory Issues

Individual Retirement Arrangements (IRAs) were enacted into law in 1974 as part of the Employee Retirement Income Security Act of 1974 (ERISA). Since the enactment of ERISA, there have been numerous changes in the statutory scheme relating to IRAs, and further changes to the existing provisions are currently being considered. Basically, IRAs refer to individual retirement accounts, individual retirement annuities, and simplified employee pensions (SEPs). It should be noted that different statutorily imposed requirements apply to each of these types of IRAs in order for the participants to obtain the tax benefits. These requirements are contained generally in §408 of the Internal Revenue Code (IRC).

Stated simply, an IRA is a vehicle whereby an employee (and a non-working spouse) can set aside a certain amount of current earnings for retirement purposes (subcategories of IRAs, employer IRAs and SEPs are employer plans established pursuant to §408 of the IRC). The amount set aside is not subject to current federal income taxation, i.e., the amount of the contribution in a particular taxable year is deductible from the individual's gross income for tax purposes. In addition, income earned on contributions is not subject to current income taxation. The IRA vehicle permits tax deferral with the contributions and income earned thereon being subject to taxation upon *distribution* to the beneficiary.

BASIC STATUTORY REQUIREMENTS FOR IRAs

The following sets forth a basic overview of the statutory requirements for the different types of IRAs. The laws relating to IRAs are extremely technical and are therefore beyond the scope of the topic, "regulatory issues affecting self-directed IRAs offered by financial services providers." However, a broad understanding of the basic requirements of IRAs is necessary before the concept of self-directed IRAs can be explored.

49

Individual Retirement Accounts

The basic statutory requirements for an individual retirement account are contained in §408 of the IRC [§408 (a) in the case of a "trustee" account and §408(h) in the case of a "custodial" account].

Pursuant to §408(a), the term "individual retirement account" means a trust created or organized in the United States for the exclusive benefit of an individual or his or her beneficiaries. Section 408(h) of the IRC permits creation and use of a "custodial" account. In order to qualify, the *written*, governing instrument creating the trust (or custodial account) must meet the following requirements:

- The written trust or custodial agreement must expressly limit "nonrollover" contributions to $2,000 per taxable year (to be deductible for a given tax year, the contribution must be made no later than the owner's tax due date).
- The trustee or custodian must be a bank or a similarly qualified person or institution.
- No part of the trust or custodial funds shall be invested in life insurance contracts.
- The interest of the individual and the balance of his or her account must be nonforfeitable.
- The written trust or custodial agreement must prohibit the commingling of the account's assets with any other property (it should be noted, however, that an exception applies in the case of "common trust funds" and "common investment funds").
- Distributions must commence no later than the taxable year in which the owner becomes 70-1/2 years of age; distributions can commence after age 59-1/2 without penalties.

Individual Retirement Annuities

Several different rules apply to individual retirement annuities (which also include endowment contracts). These rules are set forth as follows:

- The annuity contract or endowment contract must be issued by an insurance company.
- The contract must not be transferable by the owner; the entire interest of the owner must be nonforfeitable.
- The annual premium cannot be *fixed*; however, it cannot exceed $2,000 in any taxable year.
- The contract must provide that premium refunds will be used to acquire additional benefits or to pay future premiums.
- Distribution must commence no later than the taxable year in which the owner becomes 70-1/2 years of age.

Simplified Employee Pensions (SEPS)

The Revenue Act of 1978 permits employers to establish simplified employee pensions [the IRC provisions relating to SEPs are contained generally in §408(k)]. Under §408(k), a SEP is defined as an "individual retirement account" or "individual retirement annuity" which meets the criteria set forth in that section. Accordingly, the requirements relating to individual retirement accounts and annuities are incorporated into the SEP provisions. The following sets forth generally the SEP requirements of IRC §408(k):

Participation Requirements. Generally, the SEP qualifies for a calendar year only if for such year the employer contributes to the SEP for each employee who: (a) has attained the age of 25 years, *and* (b) has performed service for the employer during at least three of the immediately preceding five calendar years.

Contributions Must Not Discriminate in Favor of Certain Individuals. The SEP must not discriminate in favor of an officer, shareholder, self-employed individual, or those who are highly compensated. Employer contributions will be considered discriminatory unless they bear a uniform relationship to total compensation (not in excess of the first $200,000) of each employee maintaining a simplified employee pension.

Withdrawals Must Be Permitted. The employee must be entitled to withdraw contributions.

The following sets forth the deductions available to the employer. SEP contributions for a calendar year are deductible "for the taxable year with which or within which the calendar year ends." IRC §404(h)[g]. "Contributions made within three-and-one-half months after the close of a calendar year are treated as if they were made on the last day of such calendar year if they are made on account of such calendar year." IRC §404(h)[g](1)(B). Pursuant to IRC §404(h)[g](1)(C), "the amount deductible in a taxable year for a simplified employee pension shall not exceed 15 percent of the compensation paid to the employees during the calendar year ending with or within the taxable year." Contributions in excess of this amount are deductible in subsequent years subject, however, to the 15 percent limitation.

An employee must include an employer SEP contribution in his or her gross income for tax purposes. However, the employee is generally entitled to a deduction for the amount of the employer contribution (this assumes that the SEP qualifies as a SEP under the IRC). This deduction is generally limited to the lesser of: (a) 15 percent of the compensation from the employer which is includable in the employee's gross income (without

52

regard to the employer contributions), or (b) $30,000. It should be noted that there are certain technical exceptions to this rule which would further restrict the amount deductible by the employee.

As mentioned previously, this discussion of the general requirements of IRAs is not to be viewed as a compilation of all the technical requirements which have an impact on a "qualified" IRA program. Special rules apply for spousal IRAs as well as IRAs for certain divorced individuals. Special rules also apply to "rollover" contributions into an IRA or another IRA. An intricate set of rules also applies to early or excessively deferred withdrawals, as well as excessive contributions to an IRA. Finally, there are certain "prohibited transaction" rules which, if violated, may disqualify the IRA. As a result, the IRA may lose its tax sheltered status, and the total amount thereof may be deemed to be "distributed" for federal income tax purposes.

SELF-DIRECTED IRAs

What is a Self-Directed IRA?

A self-directed IRA is an IRA in which the owner directs the trustee/custodian to invest the assets in a particular manner; the owner also has the authority to require the trustee/custodian to dispose of particular investments and to use the proceeds to acquire new investments requested by the owner. IRA funds can be invested in stocks, bonds, mutual funds, annuities, endowment contracts, savings accounts, certificates of deposit, participations in common trust funds, and real estate. The list of possible investments is *almost* limitless. However, there are a few investments which are prohibited for a self-directed IRA. As mentioned previously, IRA contributions cannot be invested in life insurance contracts. IRA funds cannot be invested in collectibles such as precious metals, jewels, coins, stamps, antique rugs, or works of art. The only other limits are those which are self-imposed by a particular custodian/trustee or externally imposed upon a particular custodian/trustee by laws or regulations promulgated thereto (such as those applicable to particular types of financial institutions).

Self-Directed IRAs Offered by Insurance Companies

As mentioned previously, an individual retirement annuity *must* be *issued* by an *insurance company*. This does not mean, however, that the annuity must be *sold* by an insurance company. Many securities firms have insurance agency affiliates and/or are otherwise affiliated in some way with an underwriter of annuities. Many savings and loan associations are also affiliated with agents authorized to sell annuities. Often, however, state laws prohibit the affiliation of financial institutions and insurance agencies. Most commercial banks are prohibited from owning an insurance agency.

Generally, an annuity is a guaranteed series of payments to be made to the annuitant (the owner of the annuity) commencing on a certain date. If the payments are to be made for life, the annuity is called a "life income" annuity. Annuities may provide for payments for a specified minimum number of years or for a fixed number of years. Many annuity underwriters offer fixed rate annuities and a variety of variable rate annuities. Many insurance companies offer IRA variable rate annuity contracts which can be funded through different types of investment funds established by the company. Offering different types of funds provides the contributor with some discretion in regard to the manner in which his or her IRA contribution will be invested. For instance, the primary objective of one "stock fund" may be to invest primarily in common stocks traded on national securities exchanges. The primary objective of another stock fund may be to invest in the stocks of smaller companies traded in the over-the-counter market (such investments can be riskier but also can produce a high rate of return).

Generally, the funds offered through insurance companies are diversified, open-end investment companies registered under the Investment Company Act of 1940. An affiliate of the insurance company will serve as the "investment adviser" to the funds (an investment advisory agreement is usually entered into between the affiliated parties). Since investment advice is provided, the affiliated investment adviser must be registered as an investment adviser pursuant to the Investment Adviser's Act of 1940.

The insurance company usually charges an annual maintenance or administrative fee in connection with the IRA annuity. In addition, the company receives fees from the funds for providing investment advice. Brokerage commissions are also paid to brokers that handle securities transactions on behalf of the funds. Such brokers may also be affiliates of the insurance company. It should be noted, however, that the broker affiliate is generally prohibited from receiving brokerage commissions unless the commissions are "fair and reasonable" when compared to the commissions charged by unaffiliated brokers in regard to similar transactions involving similar securities during a comparable period of time. Rule 17e-1 of the SEC. Another SEC rule states that the affiliated broker may be paid for effecting securities transactions on an exchange on which it is a member *only* if the floor execution is by a broker that is not an associated person of the affiliated broker, and the affiliated broker may retain commissions in such transactions only if there is a contract with the funds permitting the affiliated broker to be paid. Usually such agreements exist among the affiliates.

Self-Directed IRAs Offered by Securities Firms

Many securities firms have sought and obtained approval from the IRS to act as custodians of IRAs. Such firms have been and continue to be intricately involved in the marketing of self-directed IRAs. They offer the investor a wide array of investment options including, but not limited to stocks, bonds, limited partnership interests, treasury bills and notes, and mutual funds. Although securities firms cannot issue FDIC or FSLIC insured certificates of deposit directly, many securities firms permit the IRA owner to direct the custodian to invest in financial institution certificates of deposit. These financial institutions are often affiliated with the securities firm, i.e., they are savings and loan associations or are banks which do not meet the definition of "bank" for purposes of the Bank Holding Company Act.

The mutual fund options operate in practically the same manner as the funds offered by insurance companies, i.e., the securities firm or an affiliate is an investment adviser to the fund; another affiliate effectuates brokerage transactions on behalf of the fund.

Self-Directed IRAs Offered by Commercial Banks

Regulation of Banks. Commercial banks are chartered as "national" banks or "state" banks. National banks are regulated by the Office of the Comptroller of the Currency (OCC). Their deposits are insured by the Federal Deposit Insurance Corporation (FDIC). *All* national banks are *members* of the Federal Reserve System.

State chartered banks are organized under state law and are subject to supervision by and must comply with the rules and regulations promulgated by the appropriate state banking department. In practically all cases, the deposits of state chartered commercial banks are insured by the FDIC. Accordingly, state chartered banks are subject to the rules and regulations of and are further subject to examination by the FDIC. State chartered banks are not required to be members of the Federal Reserve System; however, if a state chartered bank decides to become a member bank, then it will be subject to the rules, regulations, and statutes pertaining to *member* banks.

The Glass-Steagall Banking Act of 1933. The above discussion is important because the Glass-Steagall Act restricts the ability of commercial banks and their affiliates from engaging in certain types of securities transactions. The following sets forth generally the provisions of Glass-Steagall which have an impact on the offering of self-directed IRAs by commercial banks:

Section 16 (12 U.S.C. §24): [t]he business of dealing in securities and stock by the association [national bank] shall be limited to purchasing and selling such securities and stock without recourse, solely upon the order, and for the account of, customers, and in no case for its own account, and the association shall not underwrite any issue of securities or stock: Provided, That the association [national bank] may purchase for its own account investment securities under such limitations and restrictions as the Comptroller of the Currency may by regulation prescribe ... . [it should be noted that this section also applies to *member* banks of the Federal Reserve System].

Section 20 (12 USC §377): no member bank shall be affiliated in any manner ... with any corporation, association, business trust, or other similar organization engaged principally in the issue, flotation, underwriting, public sale or distribution at wholesale or retail or through syndicate participation of stocks, bonds, debentures, notes or other securities...

Section 21 (12 U.S.C. §378): it shall be unlawful - (1) For any person, firm, corporation, association, business trust or other similar organization, engaged in the business of issuing, underwriting, selling, or distributing, at wholesale or retail, or through syndicate participation, stocks, bonds, debentures, notes, or other securities, to engage at the same time to any extent whatsoever in the business of receiving deposits subject to check or to repayment upon presentation of a passbook, certificate of deposit, or other evidence of debt, or upon request of the depositor: Provided, That the provisions of this paragraph shall not prohibit national banks or state banks or trust companies (whether or not members of the Federal Reserve System) or other financial institutions or private banks from dealing in, underwriting, purchasing and selling investment securities, or issuing securities, to the extent permitted to national banking associations by the provisions of §5136 of the Revised Statutes, as amended (U.S.C,. Title 12, §24)... [It should be noted that this restriction applies to depository institutions which would include non-member banks].

Section 32 (12 U.S.C. §78): [n]o officer, director, or employee of any corporation or unincorporated association, no partner or employee of any partnership, and no individual, primarily engaged in the issue, flotation, underwriting, public sale, or distribution, at wholesale or retail, or through syndicate participation, of stocks, bonds, or other similar securities, shall serve the same time as an officer, director, or employee of any member bank except in limited classes of cases in which the Board of Governors of the Federal Reserve System may allow such service by general regulations when in the judgment of the said Board it would unduly influence the investment policies of such member bank or the advice it gives its customers regarding investments.

Sections 16, 20, and 32 of Glass-Steagall apply only to Federal Reserve member banks (all national banks and state chartered commercial banks that choose to be members). Section 21 of Glass-Steagall, however, applies to member and non-member banks.

Discount Brokerage Activities. The provisions of sections 16, 20, and 32 of Glass-Steagall have been the focus of numerous lawsuits involving attempts by commercial banks and their affiliates to engage in various types of securities activities. After substantial litigation, Security Pacific National Bank and Union Planters National Bank were successful in obtaining the right to acquire discount brokers, i.e., brokerage firms which do not provide investment advice. The Supreme Court held that Section 16 of the Glass-Steagall Act does not prohibit the affiliation between a *member* bank and a discount broker. Since that litigation commenced, numerous other member banks have acquired discount brokers. With discount broker affiliates, member banks now have the ability to offer a greater variety of investment options to the owners of self-directed IRAs without the need of relying upon a nonaffiliated broker.

It should be noted that the Office of the Comptroller of the Currency issued a policy in regard to the purchase of securities on behalf of "trust" accounts through affiliated discount brokers. Excerpts from that circular are set forth as follows:

> [t]he general rule followed by this office is that national banks may only effect securities transactions through such an affiliated company if the transactions are performed on a non-profit basis. This would permit such transactions if a fee were imposed which covered the cost of effecting the transaction and no more. However, in such cases, the national bank would be expected to have justification in its records, showing through a detailed cost analysis that the amount of the fee which was charged was justified by the cost. Under no circumstances should the bank or its affiliate make a profit from such transactions.

> *An exception to the foregoing exists in cases where specific authority to effect transactions through the affiliate exists in the appropriate governing instrument, or local law.* In addition, in that limited number of cases where all beneficiaries of a particular fiduciary account are ascertained and competent, such transactions may be authorized by those beneficiaries.

> Finally, it should be noted that accounts which are subject to the provisions of ERISA must conform to the standards contained in that Act. It would appear that the use of an affiliated discount broker would be a prohibited transaction with a party at interest. Banks seeking an interpretation of that Act should make an appropriate request to the Department of Labor (emphasis added).

Member Bank Common Trust Funds

Insurance companies, securities firms, and their affiliates derive fee income from IRAs through set-up, maintenance, and/or administrative fees; brokerage fees and/or sales charges; and fees for providing investment advice to the funds. Member banks, however, have experienced substantial resistance from The Investment Company Institute in their attempt to offer their *own* self-directed IRA products which would allow them to receive additional fee income for providing investment advice.

In 1983, Wells Fargo Bank, N.A. (a national bank) and Bank of California, N.A. (a national bank) established common trust funds for the collective investment of IRA assets. Establishment of the funds would give IRA owners another investment choice for their IRA assets (the banks already offered certificates of deposit, money market accounts, and self-directed brokerage accounts). The banks intended to obtain fee income (based on the net asset value of each fund) for providing investment advice. The banks had registered the "units of beneficial interest" as securities under the Securities Act of 1933. The banks had further filed registration statements with the Securities and Exchange Commission to register the funds as investment companies pursuant to the Investment Company Act. [Bank common trust funds consisting of commingled IRA assets do not come within the general Investment Company Act exemption for bank trust funds; the funds are not covered by the exemption set forth in §3(a)(2) of the Securities Act relating to "bank common trust funds"].

The banks sought and obtained approval to offer the funds pursuant to their trust powers. The Comptroller ruled that the creation and operation of the funds would not violate §§16 or 21 of Glass-Steagall [12 U.S.C. §§24 and 378(a)(1)]. The Comptroller granted his approval because he believed the funds represented "the offering of a bona-fide fiduciary service expressly authorized by Congress in ERISA." Shortly thereafter, The Investment Company Institute (ICI) filed suit in the United States District Court, Northern District of California, to prevent the banks from offering the funds. *The Investment Company Institute vs. Conover*, 593 F.Supp. 846 (N.D. Cal 1984). The ICI asserted that the Comptroller's ruling authorized the banks "to create what amounts to mutual funds in violation of the prohibition against the marketing of securities by commercial banks in the Glass-Steagall Banking Act of 1933...."

Generally, a commercial bank through its trust powers has the authority to commingle trust assets and purchase investment securities therewith so long as it has received the assets for a true fiduciary purpose rather than for investment. [*Investment Co. Institute vs. Camp*, 401 U.S. 617, 638 (1971)]. Accordingly, if the funds to be commingled in the banks' proposed funds would be "received for a true fiduciary purpose rather than for investment," then the offering of the funds would not violate the for investment," then the offering of the funds would not violate the provisions of Glass-Steagall. The District Court held that the funds offered by these banks do not meet the bona-fide fiduciary requirement test set forth in *Camp*. In its reasoning, the Court stated that:

> Wells Fargo and BankCal each promote their Funds as vehicles for pooled investment. Rather than commingle the assets of pre-existing trust accounts, they seek to attract investors by promoting the advantages of particular investment portfolios in direct competition with mutual funds. Both banks offer standardized, revocable trust agreements. Wells Fargo's marketing brochure, moreover, informs potential customers that they can invest all or part of their IRA funds in the stock market through two innovative investment funds. It goes on to say: These funds are highly liquid--you can "cash in" by transferring to another Wells Fargo IRA option at any time. Each fund requires a minimum $250.00 investment--less than most mutual funds. These are no-load funds.

In conclusion, the District Court set aside the Comptroller's rulings permitting the banks to offer these funds.

If upheld, it would seem clear from this decision that member banks *cannot* aggressively advertise and market "common trust funds" for the investment of IRA assets. However, on practically the same facts, the United States District Court, District of Columbia held that Citibank has the legal authority to offer such funds. *The Investment Company Institute vs. Conover*, 596 F.Supp. 1496 (D.C. 1984). In its ruling the Court stated that:

> The distinction drawn in *Camp*, between fiduciary purpose and investment, form the crux of the holding in *Investment Company Institute vs. Conover, et al*, No. 84-0742 (slip op. N.D. Cal. August 28, 1984) (ICI). In that case, plaintiff was challenging a separate but identical Ruling by the Comptroller authorizing two California banks to offer the same service involved in this case. The Northern District of California found the funds in that case to be solely for the purpose of investment and invalidated the Comptroller's Ruling. Plaintiff would have this Court do the same here. However, this Court believes, with great respect for the careful analysis shown by the Court in ICI, that the conclusion there was in error. By focusing only on whether the funds in question fit into the mold of a "common trust fund," the Court in ICI failed to recognize that both Glass-Steagall and ERISA permit collective investment by banks of trust assets held either in "common trust funds" or "common investment funds." IRC §408(a)(5). Such "investment of assets" of statutory tax exempt retirement plans is a traditional banking function as evidenced by the Comptroller's own long-standing regulations, 12 C.F.R. §9.18, *et seq.* and the legislative history of ERISA.

On January 21, 1986, the United States District Court for the District of Connecticut held that the IRA collective investment fund of Connecticut Bank and Trust Company did not violate Glass-Steagall. *Investment Company Institute vs. Clark,* Fed. Bankling L. Rep. (CCH) §86, 512. The United States Court of Appeals for the Second Circuit confirmed the District Court's decision on May 2, 1986. *Investment Company Institute v. Clark,* Fed. Bankling L. Rep. (CCH) §86, 584. Thereafter, on May 20, 1986, the United States Court of Appeals for the District of Columbia Circuit affirmed the decision of the United States District Court, District of Columbia. Fed. Sec. L. Rep. (CCH) §92, 731. As stated earlier, that District Court held that Citibank's fund does not violate Glass-Steagall. To date, no opinion has been rendered from the United States Court of Appeals for this Ninth Circuit in regard to the decision of the United States District Court, Northern District of California. As stated earlier, that District Court held that the IRA "collective trust funds" of Wells Fargo Bank N.A. and Bank of California, N.A., violated Glass-Steagall.

Until there is a definitive resolution of these conflicting opinions, it is uncertain whether member banks have the authority to market collective investment funds which could compete effectively with mutual funds.

State Non-Member Banks

State non-member banks have the power to own "discount" brokers. FDIC General Counsel Opinion No. 6, May 23, 1983.

As mentioned previously, Section 21 is the only provision of Glass-Steagall which applies to state non-member banks. This section generally prohibits a depository institution from engaging in the securities business. However, the FDIC has determined that this prohibition does not apply to a "bona-fide subsidiary" of a state non-member bank. Pursuant to its rulemaking authority, the FDIC has adopted a regulation addressing the permissible affiliation between a state non-member bank and a subsidiary security firm as well as the permissible scope of such activities. Of course, since state non-member banks are creatures of state law, the authority to own and operate a securities firm subsidiary must also comply with each bank's state law. A copy of the FDIC's release is located in the 1984-1985 Transfer Binder, CCH Fed. Banking L. Rep., paragraph 90,331. Although the regulation contains various restrictions which will limit the activities of non-member bank securities subsidiaries, this regulation permits such subsidiaries to offer "mutual funds." This will allow non-member banks to compete more efficiently and effectively with securities firms and insurance companies in the self-directed IRA market.

Savings and Loan Associations

Because savings and loan associations are not "member banks," Sections 16, 20, and 32 of Glass-Steagall do not apply to them. The only section of Glass-Steagall which could even be construed to apply to savings and loan associations is Section 21; however, as previously discussed in regard to non-member banks, the prohibitions of Section 21 can be avoided by conducting securities activities through service corporation subsidiaries. In this regard, the Federal Home Loan Bank Board (FHLBB) has approved applications by federally chartered savings and loan associations to acquire or own securities brokerage firms. As in the case of state chartered banks, state chartered savings and loan associations must be authorized by state law in order to own such subsidiaries engaging in securities activities.

It should be noted that subsidiaries of federally chartered savings and loan associations are authorized by the FHLBB to engage in certain insurance agency activities on a preapproved basis (federal savings and loan associations can own a subsidiary that has the authority to sell annuities). Since state chartered savings and loan associations are creatures of state law, state law will determine if their subsidiaries possess similar authority. It should also be noted that the FHLBB's approval of service corporation insurance agency activities does not preempt state laws in this area. Accordingly, the subsidiary must be licensed as an "insurance agent" pursuant to state law, and if a particular state's laws prohibit the affiliation of financial institutions and insurance agencies, then the savings and loan association would be prohibited from affiliating with an insurance agency.

Exchange Act Rule 3b-9

Exchange Act Rule 3b-9 became effective on January 1, 1986. This rule has had an immediate impact upon the securities activities of banks that:

- Publicly promote internalized brokerage business for transaction-related compensation;
- Receive transaction-related compensation for providing brokerage services for trust, managing agent, or other accounts to which the bank provides advice; or,
- Engage in the business of dealing in or underwriting securities.

According to Rule 3b-9, any of these activities must be conducted through a *registered broker-dealer* as of January 1, 1986. There are certain exceptions and exemptions to the rule (such as a *de minimus* exception which permits up to 1,000 transactions a year without registering), and the Securities and Exchange Commission has reserved the authority to exempt bank related securities activities "which the Commission deems not within the intended meaning and purpose of Rule 3b-9." The American Bankers Association (ABA) has vigorously sought to invalidate Rule 3b-9 on the basis that the Securities and Exchange Act of 1934 exempts banks from broker-dealer registration. The ABA sought an injunction to prevent the January 1, 1986 implementation of the rule; however, the ABA was unsuccessful. The ABA then sought an expedited appeal to the appropriate United States Court of Appeals, and that request was also denied. Accordingly, it may be quite some time until the ABA's challenge of Rule 3b-9 is decided. In the meantime, the Securities and Exchange Commission has implemented Rule 3b-9. With Rule 3b-9 in effect, banks must become registered as broker/dealers (or form registered broker-dealer subsidiaries) or change their mode of doing business to avoid registration (such as entering into networking arrangements with registered broker/dealers) if they intend to implement or continue to offer self-directed IRA programs on an efective and profitable basis.

CONCLUSION

Commercial banks, savings institutions, insurance companies, and securities firms each possess certain advantages and disadvantages in regard to their abilities to compete in the self-directed IRA market on a profitable basis.

Financial institutions are the only entities that can offer directly insured certificates of deposit, whereas insurance companies are the only entities permitted to underwrite annuities. However, affiliations and joint ventures among different types of financial service providers permit certain entities (such as commercial banks) to offer their customers a broad range of investments for their self-directed IRAs. Through planning and proper structuring of a self-directed IRA program, commercial banks, savings institutions, insurance companies, securities firms, and affiliates of these firms can compete effectively and profitably in this growing market.

Investment Strategies and Product Mix

In manufacturing a self-directed IRA, a number of choices must be made. Should a broker/dealer be established, or should a bank seek to work with an existing broker/dealer? Should the product menu be limited, to simplify customer choice, or should the investment strategy be left entirely to the discretion of the customer?

The two articles in this section represent different alternatives. Gerald Kerns describes a broker/dealer created specifically to network with a group of different depository institutions. The product menu presented to most customers is controlled, to reduce complexity in investment decision, administration, and reporting. The trust services are similarly packaged to permit a depository institution to enter the field with maximum speed and minimum cost.

A different strategy is presented in the article by Kerry Killinger. Washington Mutual Savings Bank has sought to pursue an acquisitions strategy to obtain the capacities required to compete in a broad range of financial products and services. An aggressive self-directed IRA marketing program by Washington Mutual has expanded the entire IRA base and generated substantial fee income, while simultaneously increasing the amount of deposits in IRA certificates. This strong strategy has permitted Washington Mutual to maintain a leading market share in its geographical market, competing successfully against several larger commercial banks also in the same market.

These two chapters begin the transition of the book into case studies. The authors were invited to participate with certain distinctions drawn. Each was encouraged to discuss his or her business experiences, which necessitated discussion of each one's particular business approaches and companies. At the same time, they were reminded that the purpose of this work was to contribute to industry knowledge, not promote a particular company's business objectives. This distinction is generally best upheld when the author is willing to reveal the details and the numbers, the success, and the failure of their particular endeavors. The authors in this section set a good standard in this regard.

5.   Order Instead of Chaos: Structuring a Self-Directed IRA Marketing Program

How do you control a self-directed IRA program that offers the participant everything that appears in the pages of the *Wall Street Journal*? It's hard to do, so one of the challenges is to bring order out of this chaos and still present meaningful options for the participant who wants the chance to make his retirement fund grow faster.

The typical client of a bank or thrift is not attuned to the kind of wide open investment choice that is available through brokerages, yet we see the decline of the certificate of deposit in an environment where rates are falling and many IRA accounts have reached $8,000-$10,000.

What's the answer?

For one thing, the CD or savings account with federal insurance will always be an attractive choice, regardless of rate. We're talking about decline, not disappearance. But the individual bank or thrift is well advised today to go beyond the limits of its own accounts in competing with all those other financial providers who promote the potential for faster growth.

Whether the institution's strategy is essentially offensive or defensive, there is a way to use the self-directed option. You can be as aggressive as you want to be, while making available to your customers a diverse set of choices for their funds.

Complications arise, because in order to achieve this goal you must include securities products. However, there are a number of ways for a financial institution to make securities available to the public and still receive these important benefits:

•Generate substantial fee income;
•Stop the drain of IRA dollars to stockbrokers and insurance agents;
•Offer expanded investment options to current customers;
•Expand the IRA portfolio with a competitive IRA offering;
•Provide quarterly consolidated investment reports for IRA customers.

One possible way to accomplish this is for the institution to form a subsidiary and incorporate it as a broker/dealer which is properly licensed. Table 5.1 illustrates the approximate costs involved in such a venture:

TABLE 5.1
Cost to Set Up Broker/Dealer

Incorporation

State Filings	$300.00	+ (dep. on state)
All Legal Fees	15,000.00	+
Two (2) Principals each requires 3 Licenses (Series 7, 24, & 63)		
Study Courses $500 x 2	1,000.00	+
NASD License Fees $250 x 2	500.00	
NASD Securities Filings	1,200.00	+
State Securities Filing Including Bonds	400.00	(dep. on state)
Consultant	7,000.00	+

Minimum cost to set up: $24,420.00
Plus
Annual cost to operate: $100,000 absolute minimum

Depending on the state of domicile, there may be some elements that vary. However, in general terms, this kind of venture will require two principals; that is, two people who have extensive experience, are licensed as principals and who can handle the securities compliance requirements. You'll also probably need a consultant or two to keep you out of regulatory difficulty.

So the approximate cost is somewhere in the neighborhood of $25,000 to set up a broker/dealer of your own. That is just the beginning, however. You'll also need a very large sales volume in order to handle ongoing costs and make your broker/dealer operation profitable.

You are facing a minimum of $100,000 a year in expenses to operate a broker/dealership. How many institutions can generate the volume of sales that would produce this kind of income?

The second possible way to participate in the securities market for the institution is to network with an existing broker/dealership. Many have done this in the discount brokerage arena. Unfortunately, the results of discount brokerage are extremely low income from the sales that do occur. Can the institution afford the disintermediation they face in order to provide their client base with securities products and receive such poor income as compensation?

Another way for you to network is to make an arrangement with a broker/dealer that does not discount. In other words, it sells loaded products. Why would you wish to sell loaded products in a self-directed IRA program? Obviously, the sale of a program requires salespeople, and salespeople have to be compensated. If the institution itself is going to be disintermediated in any sense, then it also needs compensation for the loss of the deposit. But it also needs compensation for the simple expense of making the program available.

My personal preference is to sell front-loaded securities products, so the customer knows exactly what expense he is facing when he buys the product.

There are programs around which have internal-loaded or back-loaded products. I have a problem with selling this kind of a program, because they tend to come back and bite you when the customer does an unexpected transaction, such as backing out of a program early or confronting fees that he did not really understand or didn't realize existed.

In order for you to sell the securities, it is going to be necessary that you have licensed registered representatives so you are legally offering the securities to the public. Licensed registered representatives can receive commissions for both securities and insurance products when they're properly licensed. This is obviously the way to pay for the cost of the sales expense.

This process does not involve an unreasonable expense, as Table 5.2 illustrates.

TABLE 5.2
Cost to License a Series 6 Registered Representative

NASD Registration	$ 50.00	
NASD Fingerprints	14.00	
Series 6 Exam	50.00	
Bonding Fee	20.00	
State of License Registration	25.00	(dep. on state)
Course of Study	100.00	
If the State of License has Blue Sky		
Law, add	50.00	NASD Exam
	+50.00	Course of Study
Total Cost:	$ 359.00	+ (Approx.)

Depending again on the state of domicile, there are slight variations in the requirements and type of license. But in any case, this one-time expense is minor.

Now that you're able to deliver the securities product to the public and pay a salesperson to offer the product legitimately, then what is the return and what is the method of returning fee income to the institution for a securities product under the current regulatory atmosphere?

68

FIGURE 5.1

Broker/Dealer/Bank S&L Relationship

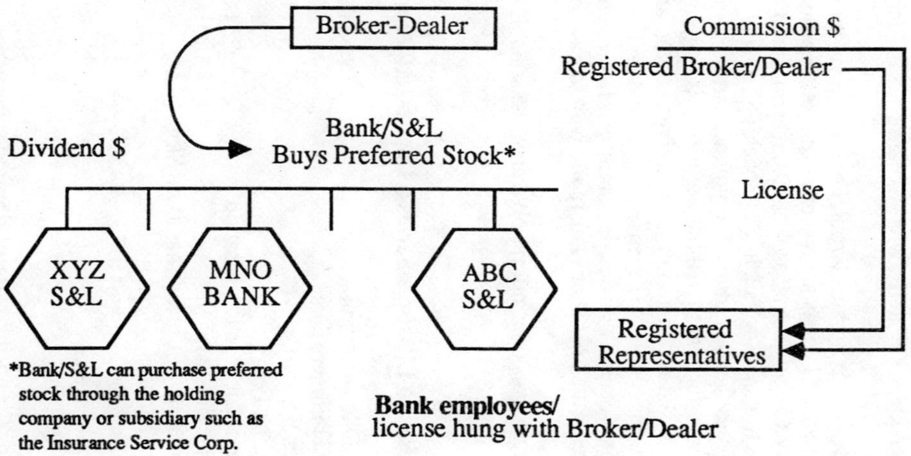

Broker-Dealer

Commission $

Registered Broker/Dealer

License

Registered Representatives

Bank/S&L Buys Preferred Stock*

Dividend $

XYZ S&L

MNO BANK

ABC S&L

Bank employees/ license hung with Broker/Dealer

*Bank/S&L can purchase preferred stock through the holding company or subsidiary such as the Insurance Service Corp.

There may be a variety of methods for doing this, but here is one illustration. It's possible for a subsidiary of the bank or savings and loan to purchase stock in a broker/dealer corporation. This could be a special series of preferred stock which would be differentiated from any other series of shares sold by that broker/dealership. The broker/dealer could then return fee income to the institution subsidiary in the form of dividends.

The particular dividend paid may be different from any other particular special series of preferred shares. The broker/dealer can also generate a commission to a licensed registered representative.

In developing a controlled self-directed IRA program, you will be seeking a product mix that offers a wide choice for the public and yet can be controlled in terms of administration, and investment reporting, and that generates liquidity.

Here is a product menu that can be the basis for a program that accomplishes those goals:

- Certificates of deposit
- Annuities
- Mutual funds (and other securities)
- Other insurance products

As the anchor of the program, the CD is clearly identified with the institution. The customer knows with whom he is dealing. It has all of the comfort and familiarity of a federally insured deposit with terms and rates that are controlled by the institution, therefore allowing the institution to be just as aggressive or defensive in the interest rate market as it may wish to be.

The second investment choice is an annuity. This is a life insurance product offered by a legal reserve life insurance company which guarantees the return of principal and interest based on its legal reserve status. The annuity is the only instrument in the country that can guarantee to the participant an income that he or she may not outlive. That is a settlement option for a lifetime income, so I feel it's an element that should be involved in every customer retirement program in the country.

So the menu includes the safety and stability of the life insurance industry in the self-directed IRA program. Another advantage of having an annuity involved in the investment mix is that the savings and loan or bank may become less eager to be interest competitive with its certificate of deposit, which allows an escape valve for the program. The customer may choose to move into a fixed return instrument that has many characteristics of a savings account but possibly can provide a superior return in certain interest rate atmospheres.

The third element suggested is the use of mutual funds. Mutual funds are a logical inclusion in a retirement program, particularly for a bank or savings and loan customer. Mutual funds are relatively conservative securities products. They are not instruments that are intended to be traded. They are long term investments, and this makes a lot of sense for your retirement program.

Mutual funds have many advantages for the customer. They are simply a pool of a lot of different investors' money, which is used by the management of the mutual fund to give tremendously broad diversification for a very small investment. In other words, the pool of money is invested in hundreds, maybe thousands of stocks of different companies for broad diversification.

The customer also gets the benefit of professional management. Most small investors do not have the time nor the inclination to manage and decide what to buy, what to sell, when to buy, when to sell, etc.

Mutual funds are liquid investments, and, in the case where "families" of funds are offered, it is possible for the customer to have free access to move from one fund to another within that family at minimal expense. This is a desirable self-direction feature.

Another very interesting menu choice is that of real estate stock funds. Real estate stock funds are specialty funds that are not the purchase of real property, but they allow the small investor to enter the real estate market with small amounts of money that are invested in corporations or entities that are involved in the real estate business. They offer liquidity. They offer professional management. They solve those problems in real estate that involve poor liquidity, difficulty of property management, and diversification.

The last item in the product menu is an immediate annuity as a benefit payment vehicle. It's a flexible modern instrument which has great merit as a payout device for a retirement plan.

Given that we have now established a sales organization and controlled menu of products, our next step is to arrange for the administration and safekeeping of the investments. The problem here is that most institutions are not in a position to provide the custodial or trustee function necessary to handle a wide diversity of investments.

Therefore, it makes sense to use an independent trust company as the custodian and trustee in a self-directed program of this type. There are several elements that should be examined when choosing a custodial trust company for this purpose.

Mainly, you want to be certain that this particular trustee never becomes your competitor for the funds deposited in the self-directed program. In other words, you should look for a trust company that is product-neutral and has nothing to sell but its services.

You also want a trustee that is a specialist in self-direction. You do not need to conduct an experiment when you get into such a complicated program, so you need to look for the experience, the capacity to administer and report and to provide benefit payment. You also want a custodial trust company which is going to provide flexible trust forms for a variety of programs, not just your IRAs, but also Keoghs and corporate plans.

Therefore, you want a custodial trust company which includes at least the following services:

•Trusteeship
•Safekeeping of assets
•Administration
•Reporting
•Benefit payments
•Product neutrality

You want the trust company to be the fiduciary and have that liability. For reporting, you want it to prepare reports, both for the government and for the customers, plus reports for your salespeople. Their benefit payments capabilities should allow for a wide variety of options, all the way from an immediate annuity to a simple liquidation of assets.

To help you understand the relationships of the different parties involved, Figure 5.2 gives an indication of the sequence of events in opening, constructing, and then operating a self-directed IRA under this format.

The customer works with a licensed registered representative to open the trust document, make investment selections, and make contributions payable to the trust company. The trust company then opens the IRA trust account, wrapping any new assets and any existing assets from other IRAs that may be transferred in. The trust company, in turn, makes account reports on a consolidated quarterly basis back to the customer and to the registered representative. After the trust company has opened the account, it makes the investments on behalf of the IRA participant in the bank or savings and loan certificates of deposit in the annuities, the mutual funds, etc.

In the test marketing that was conducted in this format, the savings and loan customer prospects were selected and obtained from a variety of sources, including maturing certificate lists, branch personnel referrals, contacts by the salesmen, and referrals by sold and satisfied customers. The interest level of the customer has been very high in the test marketing phase for this self-directed IRA menu of investment. Obviously, there is a subliminal desire to diversify the IRA investment by the participant, and, although the clamor may not be at a high level, the customer is sensitive to the fact that interest rates are down and that investment media, perhaps other than the certificate of deposit customarily used, is going to be an attractive option.

The funds have come from a variety of places including foreign IRAs that were transferred from other institutions, ranging all the way from insurance companies, stock brokerage, savings and loans, and banks. The closing ratio of presentations to sales is running at a very high level, indicating that those who exhibit interest in self-direction are prone to buy.

72

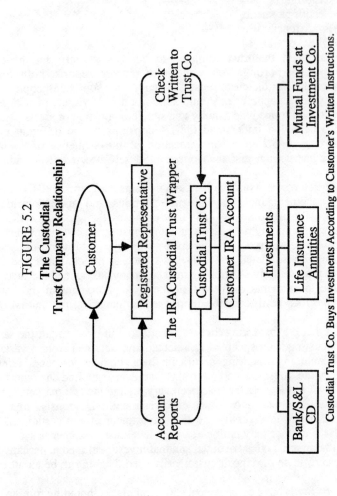

FIGURE 5.2
The Custodial
Trust Company Relationship

Customer

Registered Representative

The IRA Custodial Trust Wrapper

Check Written to Trust Co.

Custodial Trust Co.

Customer IRA Account

Account Reports

Investments

Bank/S&L CD

Life Insurance Annuities

Mutual Funds at Investment Co.

Custodial Trust Co. Buys Investments According to Customer's Written Instructions.

It's obvious that the new self-directed IRA approach is a benefit to the institution. It allows the participant to choose and change a personal investment strategy within the IRA provided by the bank or the savings and loan. It is definitely a savings acquisition vehicle which generates substantial fee income, as well. It stops the drain of IRA dollars to stockbrokers and insurance agents. It offers expanded investment options to current customers of the bank, and it expands the IRA portfolio with a competitive IRA offering. It provides a quarterly consolidated investment report for the IRA customer. All of these are very attractive features.

The fee generation potential of the product is substantial. Table 5.3 shows an example based on a third being invested in each type of product: CDs, annuities, and mutual funds. The example omits any guess at spreads on CD deposits.

TABLE 5.3
Revenue Projection

For *every* $1,000,000 of self-directed IRAs sold, *if*:

1/3 invested Cert. of Deposit	1/3 invested Annuities	1/3 invested Mut. Funds/Secur.
$333,000	$333,000	$333,000
x ? spread	x 5.5% comm.	x 4.0% avg. comm.
? profit	$ 18,315 income	$ 13,320
		- 6,660 dividend net income tax
		(50% T.B.)
		$ 6,660 income

CD   =   ?
Annuity   = $18,315.00
Mutual   =   6,660.00
              $24,975.00 income
                        If 25% of participants purchase
Completion Ins.   5,500.00 (life insurance: 25 x $22
                                premium=$5,500)
              $30,475.00

Assuming a return of 5-1/2 percent on the annuity, that area alone would generate $18,315 of income. The 1/3 invested in securities brings in $13,320, assuming a 4 percent commission--and this is eroded by dividend income tax--for a net of $6,660.

If we're successful in selling completion insurance (very low premium universal life) for 25 percent of the participants, another $5,500 would be generated, for a gross revenue of $30,475 in the first year sale of the $1 million in self-directed IRAs.

Remember that each year annual contributions will be made to all of these IRAs up to $2,000 each, so they keep generating new money and new commission income. Over time, the $1 million in IRAs will grow, due to contributions and earnings, and will reach a value of at least $5 million.

Of this resulting $5 million, more income is generated when each participant retires. Assuming only 50 percent of them purchase immediate annuities for lifetime benefits, this would result in another $137,500 of fee income to the institution.

These illustrations are realistic, and they show that the self-directed IRA is not just a defense against the brokers; it is a potent money-maker that belongs in your product mix.

The certificate of deposit savings account vehicle will always be the lead product in any conservative self-directed retirement program. The CD and the annuity contract are conservative vehicles as elements in a balanced investment mix. Those two instruments are interest-sensitive and will tend to rise and fall in value in the mix as interest rates rise and fall. When you look at the securities markets and real estate markets, they tend to do better when interest rates are low and not as well when interest rates are high. Therefore, a balanced mix of investments between certificates and annuities on the interest-sensitive side, and securities and real estate funds on the growth side, will give the customer a good balance and a long term mix that will be successful and above average in return over a long period of time. This is the type of investment program that is most suitable to the traditional customer of the savings and loan or bank.

6. Washington Mutual Financial Group

Pioneering innovative IRAs has paid off for the Washington Mutual Financial Group: It now ranks Number One in IRA assets in Washington state.

Headquartered in Seattle, Washington, the group provides banking, securities, insurance, retirement, and travel services through a state chartered savings bank and seven other affiliated companies. With a customer base of more than 250,000 households throughout Washington state, the Washington Mutual Financial Group had more than $4.8 billion in assets under management in early 1986.

Washington Mutual Savings Bank is the flagship operation, with $4.2 billion in assets and 52 branches statewide. It ranks as Washington's third largest financial institution and largest thrift. The bank converted to stock ownership in 1983.

Its self-directed IRA program grew out if its mission to be the "premier financial services organization in the Pacific Northwest." To that end, Washington Mutual strives to deliver products and services that meet the following criteria:

First, all business moves must be driven by consumer needs. As a long-established bank with a family-oriented image, Washington Mutual considers its strong relationship with its customers as its primary marketing advantage. Therefore, its marketing strategy is to meet as many as possible of its existing customers' needs by offering a broad range of financial services. These have been added within the bank's existing branches for the efficiency and convenience of "one-stop shopping." This also creates efficiencies for the Financial Group companies, which can share customers and research capabilities and save on facilities costs.

Second, as a stockholder-owned organization, the Financial Group's primary business goal is to attain the highest possible long term return for its shareholders. Therefore, it makes every effort to be on the leading edge of profitable new products and services, products it also deems

75

to be best for its customers. This double-edged effort--products and services that are best for the customer and also most profitable for the Financial Group--helped the group achieve a near-record year for profits in 1985.

Washington Mutual's highly flexible charter (state, stock form) has allowed it to expand into many areas currently off limits to most commercial banks. In 1982, Washington Mutual acquired Murphey Favre, a full-service securities brokerage, and Composite Research, a manager of six mutual funds. That same year, it also formed its own full-lines insurance agency, Washington Mutual Service Corp. In 1983 it acquired E.J. Life, an insurance underwriter. In 1984, Washington Mutual established Murphey Favre Properties, a subsidiary whose purpose is real estate syndications. In 1985, the bank acquired a major Northwest pension and actuarial consulting firm called Benefit Service Corp., and, aided by a seasoned travel agency management team, formed Mutual Travel. In 1985 Washington Mutual Savings Bank also formed a wholly-owned "downstream" holding company, WM Financial, to manage all of the subsidiary companies.

IRA HISTORY

True to its commitment to being on the leading edge of profitable new products, Washington Mutual entered the expanded IRA market of 1982 with an ambitious goal: to open 10,000 new accounts. Its 1982 IRAs were traditional bank IRAs, but with two options: fixed rate, for maturities of 18 and 30 months, and a variable-rate account dubbed the Harvest account.

It was Harvest that gave Washington Mutual a significant head start in the early months of 1982. Unlike the variable-rate IRAs offered by some other institutions, the Harvest account was not tied to a single index such as a treasury bill rate. Instead, it was tied to Washington Mutual's own portfolio of investments and offered higher interest rates. Consumers shopped around and were attracted by the high interest, FDIC-insured account.

Other features also contributed to Washington Mutual's success. The bank's customer-oriented approach dictated that procedures be streamlined to make opening an IRA as simple as possible. Quarterly IRA statements and competitively priced charges also were important to keep in step with other institutions.

But perhaps most important to the future of the program was the wide array of periodic add-to options. Customers were invited to add regularly to their IRA accounts in any one of five ways: "pay-by-phone" banking, branch deposits, payroll deductions, transmatic payments, or coupon payment books.

The success of this first-year strategy is shown in the numbers: Washington Mutual exceeded its IRA goal by more than 100 percent. The two types of accounts offered options for ever-changing economic conditions. Harvest was most popular in the first months it was offered. As interest rates in general began to rise, however, the fixed-rate IRA became more competitive as customers became eager to lock in high returns. By the end of 1982, Washington Mutual had opened 21,000 new IRA accounts, bringing the bank's total IRA assets to $70 million.

In 1983, Washington Mutual continued its traditional IRA program and booked $7 million in new IRA money. With a total of $77 million in IRA assets and 22,900 accounts, the bank then became the state leader in both number of accounts and total IRA assets. Meanwhile, Washington Mutual was busy developing its first self-directed IRA program in a joint effort with its newly-acquired full-service brokerage firm, Murphey Favre, Inc.

SELF-DIRECTED IRA

An important goal for the self-directed IRA program was to establish an economic base of accounts. It was determined that 10,000 accounts and $15 million of self-directed IRA assets were required to offset start-up and promotional expenses. To reach these volume objectives, a detailed business plan was prepared.

Washington Mutual and Murphey Favre focused on differentiating the products available within a Washington Mutual/Murphey Favre IRA, thereby differentiating their IRA from those offered by other institutions in the state. Promotional materials pointed out the availability of the full range of Washington Mutual time deposits and money market accounts, as well as a wide range of stocks, bonds, and mutual funds through Murphey Favre. Customers were not limited just to bank products or just brokerage products; they could choose investments in any combination they wished.

MARKETING STRATEGY

Marketing strategy each IRA season includes an all-out campaign using virtually every available medium. Several waves of direct mailings are sent to current and prospective customers. The Financial Group's research department has developed a composite profile of the typical Washington Mutual/Murphey Favre IRA customer, to target more accurately such direct mailings.

Media advertising focuses on half-page newspaper advertisements. These are larger than the ads of most competitors. Washington Mutual has found newspapers to be the best medium for product-oriented advertising. (It reserves television for more general, "image"-oriented advertising.) Newspaper ads focus on Washington Mutual/Murphey Favre's number one position in IRAs, and include boxes with rates for both bank and brokerage products. For cost effectiveness, newspaper advertising is "pulsed," with maximum placements at the beginning and end of the IRA season.

Every opportunity to promote IRAs within the branches and in customer statements also is exploited. Statement stuffers are mailed out to approximately 200,000 existing customers between March 1 and April 15. Branch lobby posters, window banners, counter cards, and teller receipts also support the IRA campaign. Each echoes the "number one in IRAs" and "choices" themes. Branches also are supplied with lists of current IRA customers and phone numbers for reminder phone calls. Priority customers are listed according to IRA balance and age when possible, to help branches determine their best prospects.

In addition, a bonus interest campaign was introduced with the self-directed IRA in 1984. The original program, a flat $10 in bonus interest for IRA contributions of $1,000 or higher, was expanded in following years to give additional incentive for rollovers and transfers. A sliding scale bonus program now offers $25 to $2,500 in bonus interest for rollovers or transfers of $5,000 to $500,000.

Existing IRA customers receive special attention through a quarterly IRA newsletter begun in 1985. The newsletters cover current news related to IRAs and reinforce the message of Washington Mutual/Murphey Favre IRA options. The Financial Group's marketing department also develops thank-you letters for customers who have opened or added to an IRA. The letters are personalized by branch and are automatically generated by the computer system.

DELIVERY SYSTEMS

Washington Mutual/Murphey Favre self-directed IRAs are sold through three channels: Murphey Favre registered representatives, bank branch employees, and the bank's telemarketing department.

Murphey Favre employs 70 registered representatives, of which 52 are regularly stationed within Washington Mutual's 52 branches. The remainder operate out of six free-standing Murphey Favre offices.

Washington Mutual has 52 branches across the state. During the IRA promotion, each branch designates one outstanding employee as the resident IRA specialist. This employee is responsible for honing his or her knowledge of IRA options, sales techniques, and cross-selling skills. The branch IRA specialist and Murphey Favre representative work together to cross-sell products as appropriate to the customer's needs.

In addition, the bank's telemarketing department is playing an increasing role in IRA information and sales. The telemarketing phone number appears in all newspaper ads and IRA newsletters and has proven a convenient option for IRA customers. 1985 afforded a special opportunity for telemarketing when the April 14 deadline happened to fall on a Monday. An IRA hotline was established to open accounts over the weekend, with customers delivering their deposits to the night drop at their nearest branch. The hotline was publicized by radio and newspaper advertisements.

The marketing staff prepares sales tips for each of these delivery groups after carrying out comparison shopping of competing institutions. This knowledge helps front-line employees develop their strongest competitive sales approach.

Employees also are reminded of sales essentials, such as techniques of closing a sale, by means of special sales updates and "tip cards" provided for quick reference.

OPERATIONS

The Washington Mutual/Murphey Favre self-directed IRA requires two operational systems: For customers selecting only bank products, the operating system of Washington Mutual is utilized; for customers selecting securities products or a combination of securities and bank products, the Murphey Favre operating system is used. This approach required minimal modifications to either system, so costs and time delays were avoided.

RESULTS

Washington Mutual has retained its position as Washington state's leader in IRA assets since 1983. In 1984, the first year for the Washington Mutual/Murphey Favre self-directed account, combined IRA assets reached $170 million ($98 million in bank products, $72 million in securities). 1985 saw even greater growth, with $123 million in bank products, and $91 million in securities, for a total of $214 million in IRA assets.

Number of accounts increased to 37,800 in 1984 and 47,200 by mid-1985. By 1985, the average account size was $4,533.

The overall mix of assets among IRA accounts held with Washington Mutual/Murphey Favre is divided almost evenly between bank and brokerage products, with slightly more going to bank products. Time deposits account for 53 percent, while 4 percent consists of money market accounts. Mutual funds attract 22 percent of the money, while the remaining 21 percent is invested in individual securities. Among mutual funds, government and corporate bond funds are the most popular with IRA investors, with 51 percent of IRA mutual fund money going to them. Of the remainder invested in mutual funds, 27 percent is in growth funds, and 22 percent in balanced funds.

Washington Mutual's IRA leadership is particularly remarkable when viewed in relation to total assets. Its closest competitor, Seattle First National Bank, holds $30 million less in IRA assets, yet has total assets more than twice Washington Mutual's.

TABLE 6.1
Market Position
as of 4/26/85
(in millions)

	IRA Assets	Total Assets
Washington Mutual	$199	$4,000
Seattle First	169	9,000
Peoples	117	2,300
Rainier	94	7,600
First Interstate	70	3,000

OBSERVATIONS

Washington Mutual views the profitability of its self-directed IRA product to date as "adequate." It is definitely profitable, and growth in accounts and assets assures future profitability.

Strategy for 1986 focuses on improving profitability by working to retain existing accounts, targeting additions to existing accounts, and targeting banks and brokers for rollovers and transfers.

Profitability aside, the self-directed IRA fits in well with Washington Mutual's products, which typically include unique, recognizable products and a wide range of choices. Murphey Favre also has found that the promotion of self-directed IRAs increases awareness of its capabilities and attracts non-IRA investment business such as deferred annuities, universal life insurance and tax-free bonds.

In summary, the self-directed IRA has allowed Washington Mutual to capture increased market share at a time when most thrifts have been losing share of IRA deposits. The product is desired by the consumer and is profitable to the organization.

Case Studies

Moving from theory to practice is generally a learning experience continued through testing. Especially with a new product, such as the self-directed IRA, initial product configurations may require substantial market experience before the finally accepted variations are fully obvious. What can be learned from the initial efforts is the strategic planning, which has formed the theory, and the preliminary results gleaned from the market.

In the first chapter of this section, Connie Matsui shares the efforts of Wells Fargo Bank, an institution which could boast over $1 billion in IRA balances and over 100,000 IRA customers even before it acquired Crocker Bank. Wells is also noteworthy for the extent to which it has developed its own investment management expertise, discount brokerage services, and trust administration capabilities.

Even a quick examination of Jerry Fitzwater's chapter makes clear a further development of policy. Union Bank has pursued a strategy where the self-directed IRA products and services developed by the bank have been converted to a "turn-key" package designed to permit other financial institutions to offer self-directed accounts to their customers. This type of market positioning can seek to utilize advantages of scale wherein the larger institutions devote the development, talent, time, and capital required to manufacture the required system components, thereby recovering costs and increasing revenue through the downstream sharing of these facilities with other institutions unwilling or unable to make a similar program investment. Fitzwater's chapter is also noteworthy for its comments regarding the extension of the IRA market to customers who have not yet taken advantage of this tax-qualified retirement savings plan.

Finally, Paul Werlin illustrates the alternative strategy of developing the self-directed systems, again for use by multiple financial institutions, but here without the requirement that the systems used belong to a financial institution's competitor. Werlin's discussion highlights the flexibility of the joint venture structure by discussing the adaptation of the INVEST program to the different marketing and advertising requirements of two subscribing client banks.

7. Case Study: Wells Fargo Bank

Much has been said about IRA markets and marketing, and not enough about *long term strategy* and product enhancement and development.

It may be useful to start by describing where Wells Fargo's IRA program stood two years ago. Like many other banks and savings and loans, Wells Fargo had enjoyed enormous success with the universalization of IRAs for all working people in 1981. In fact, due to its extensive investment in training and in marketing materials, Wells Fargo captured *more* than its share of the emerging IRA market. While we did offer a broader array of insured time deposit options than most of our competitors, ultimately we perceived that it was the clarity and accessibility of our product and people that set us apart, not the investments.

At that time, investment selection just did not seem critical to our average customer. Most of our customers were most concerned about safety and security of their retirement funds. Also, because IRA rules and regulations were new and somewhat intimidating, it appeared that consumers wanted to stick with investments that they were already familiar with--like time deposits with guaranteed rates and terms--rather than venture into totally uncharted territory. Given the long term nature of the IRA, the longest term options had the greatest appeal, probably because they offered higher rates as well.

Today, the vast majority of Wells Fargo's customers still prefer to invest in traditional insured deposits, both term as well as liquid money market accounts. However, in analyzing our deposit outflows and in tracking competitive trends, we now know that insured deposits alone can neither retain all our current customers nor attract new customers. All one has to do is look at the increasing share of the market being taken away from banks and thrifts by brokers and mutual funds in just the past year or two, to realize that a self-directed investment program is an important addition to an institution's IRA portfolio.

83

84

Even though the term self-directed is familiar, individual definitions
vary. For many, "self-directed" refers primarily to a brokerage account
where the IRA investor is free to choose from whatever his or her broker has
available. This may include stocks and bonds, government securities, zero
coupon bonds, and mutual funds, as well as certificates of deposit. This
broad definition of self-directed will be used here to mean access to a whole
spectrum of investment vehicles, much as you would find through a full-
service brokerage account or trust account relationship, not just about the
trading of stocks and bonds within an IRA.

It is important to think of a self-directed account as broadly as
possible, because that is where the consumer is driving us. As the
accumulated balance in the average IRA account approaches $10,000,
individual account holders realize that:

- They now have enough money to diversify their previous "safe and
  sound" investment strategy;
- They need to take the allocation of this money seriously, particularly
  as retirement savings grow larger and larger relative to their non-tax-
  sheltered savings;
- They realize that they are viewed as highly attractive customers by
  nearly every financial institution in existence, all of whom are
  scrambling all over each other to gain that prized IRA relationship.

Of course, if a particular account holder has received a sizeable
payout from an employer's pension plan or owns a small business, he or she
knows that this substantial retirement savings gives him or her even greater
leverage in the marketplace. In short, the consumer has become "choosy,"
some of us might say "fickle."

Several other external factors have contributed to this heightened
consumer awareness and the warlike nature of the marketplace. Much to
banks' and thrifts' dismay, interest rates just haven't been what they used to
be over the past two years, and while there still are institutions out there
buying market share with double-digit interest rates, the 14 percent to 16
percent rates being paid in 1981 and 1982 are long gone. Customers lured
into IRAs at those rates are less likely to settle for the 8 to 9 percent yields of
today.

At the same time, the stock market has been performing beyond
expectations. Even the most skittish investor cannot overlook the
tremendous gains of the past two years nor the current ease of entry via
mutual funds of every size, shape, flavor, and form. And as newspapers
and magazines tout the latest trend in IRA investing--whether it be zero
coupon bonds, GNMA funds, or a socially responsible mutual fund--
heretofore cautious investors have learned to question the standard bank
lineup of investment choices. This skepticism has, in turn, been accelerated
by the fusillade of aggressive advertising and personal sales efforts brokers
have targeted at the IRA investor.

As a result, any financial institution with more than a short term commitment to the market must seek ways of giving the choosy investor what he or she is looking for.   There are a number of expansion opportunities, but probably the most common method of expanding your IRA investment portfolio is to allow IRA customers access to brokerage services. Of 300 leading financial institutions surveyed by TransData Corp. in 1985, approximately 48 percent offered self-directed IRA brokerage accounts. Banks and thrifts have structured these brokerage services in a variety of ways: purchasing turn-key investment services through a discount broker and/or fund manager, extending their own internal brokerage operations to accommodate IRA investors, or building or buying a brokerage subsidiary. Brokerage operations clearly open up the stock, bond, and money markets to the individual who wants to make his or her own investment choices. Access to mutual funds and/or collective investment funds has been somewhat more circuitous and has depended on the funds desired as well as the given regulatory climate.

Again, many banks and thrifts have chosen to rely on an outside party to deliver investment fund expertise, in the form of either well-known "name" funds or a "private label." Some banking institutions, Citibank being one of them, have decided to utilize their in-house pension fund managers to deliver the same sort of pooled stock or bond investments to their IRA bases. This mode has been approved for banks by the Comptroller of the Currency as well as by the SEC, but has been challenged in court by the Investment Company Institute, the trade association for the mutual fund industry. At present, two decisions *for* bank collective funds for IRA and one *against* bank collective funds for IRA are being weighed in the Federal Appeals Court. Only time will tell the outcome, but the push for expanded investments is evident.

Assuming that these environmental and consumer pressures are industry-wide, how do you decide which strategic alternative is right for your organization? Like most things, it comes down to profitability. There are some institutions which justify the IRA as a loss leader for the sake of tying the customer into a long term relationship which they hope can be expanded into other products which do generate profits. However, this belief can never be sustained, primarily because IRA balances simply aren't as stable as they used to be.

IRA investors are becoming less and less complacent, especially those with larger accounts and who tend to be more sophisticated and more in touch with the broad financial community. The industry's zealous marketing efforts have, fortunately or unfortunately, taught consumers to shop around for a home for their IRA. As long as this competition exists an institution cannot take its current balances for granted. Moreover, for long term viability, an IRA portfolio must be profitable on a stand-alone basis. In this age of shrinking margins on all financial services, no financial institution can afford to support a money-losing product, even for the sake of positioning.

86

The choice to offer a self-directed account must be based on sustained, if not substantially increased, profitability from an IRA portfolio. So the objectives in establishing a self-directed IRA program are simple: to increase margins and to create new sources of income.

To increase margins, one must look at both sides of the profit picture, costs as well as revenues. For instance, you should ask yourself questions like: Have your costs per IRA been increasing or decreasing over the past few years? Or more basically, Do you know what your acquisition and maintenance costs per account are? Can you economically support increased growth in the number *and* complexity of IRAs? Are you prepared to make the initial outlay required for start-up expenses for legal, marketing, and programming expertise? In addition, what are the costs of converting existing balances to self-directed investments, both over the shortterm as well as the long term? Can you afford to give up the spread income you make on current deposits? This last question can only be answered "yes" if you have intelligently priced your self-directed account. This is where creating new sources of income comes in.

Instead of relying solely on net funds to support a traditional IRA portfolio, an expanded IRA investment program offers considerable potential for fee income in addition to spread. Fee income can be generated in many forms, depending on the structure of the self-directed account; for instance, institutions may charge account setup fees, annual maintenance fees, transaction fees and/or share in brokerage commissions and investment management fees, and their products can still remain competitively priced.

At the same time, incremental business will be gained from new customers who would otherwise not have been attracted to your IRA program. Even though these individuals may not necessarily invest initially in stocks, bonds, or funds, the fact that these options are available through the same institution will have a stabilizing effect on your portfolio and a healthy effect on your profits.

Consequently, from a strategic standpoint the profitability of self-directed accounts gives your organization three important benefits:

•A way to supplement shrinking spreads with hard-dollar income;
•A way to be indifferent to the changing mix of deposit versus investment balances;
•A way to ensure financial durability over the long run.

Ultimately, it was these three factors which shaped Wells Fargo's strategic plan three years ago. The following paragraphs summarize the key points in Wells Fargo's reasoning and experience in choosing a self-directed investment program.

Amidst threats of saturated markets and encroachment by non-bank competitors, we began in 1983 to evaluate seriously our commitment to the IRA marketplace. We did preliminary marketing and profitability analyses and found that we had the raw material to carve out a significant share of the California IRA market. We already had investment management expertise in-house through Wells Fargo Investment Advisors, the largest index fund manager in the country. We also had established a discount brokerage facility over a year ago in cooperation with Donaldson, Lufkin and Jenrette. And, most importantly, our retirement programs area was in the process of converting from an expensive outside data processor to a highly *flexible, dedicated* retirement accounting computer system within Wells Fargo.

After about two months of detailed analysis, we gained senior management approval to tie all of these resources together into one comprehensive package in time for the 1983-1984 IRA selling season. We call this package the Next Stage IRA; currently three major investment categories are offered:

- Insured deposits, including five term-deposit options, as well as an insured money market option;
- Investment funds, comprised of two index funds managed by Wells Fargo Investment Advisors, one based on the Standard and Poor's 500 and the second based on the universe of small companies on the New York Stock Exchange;
- Discount brokerage services through which individual investors can purchase a variety of corporate and government securities at substantially reduced commissions.

Because of our state-of-the-art accounting system, we also offer the convenience of all these investments under a single account number and on a consolidated account statement. Best of all, our modular system gives us the ability to track accurately investment selections, inflows and outflows as well as customer demographics. This enables us to monitor and refine constantly our long-range strategy to meet the changing needs of the IRA investor.

Wells Fargo believes that the future of the IRA business lies with those institutions which can be flexible in their approach to the market, can react quickly to competitive trends, and are willing to continue to make investments in preserving and increasing their market share. This formula has worked for us to the point where we now have over $1 billion in IRA balances and over 180,000 IRA customers (exclusive of volume from the recently announced merger with Crocker Bank).

Finally, it's important to review the key points in making the strategic decision to offer a self-directed IRA. Because each organization has a unique situation, these points are phrased in the form of questions to be answered according to your institution's needs.

First, what have been your organization's primary strengths and weaknesses in competing for IRA business? For instance, looking at your own portfolio and sales network, do you see need for concern or improvement? By looking at your outbound transfers and withdrawals, do you know why deposits are leaving you and/or are attracted to you?

Second, what are the resources available to support a self-directed IRA program? In Wells Fargo's case it had much of the expertise it needed in-house. Smaller institutions may not have this advantage and are instead forced to buy these services from outside parties. These smaller firms may, in fact save a substantial amount of start-up expense but over the long term may also forgo increasing share of income and increasing economies of scale as their portfolio grows.

Third, assuming you have senior management approval to support a long term IRA strategy (admittedly a big assumption when institutions are worried about overall profitability not just IRA profitability) do you have control over the direction of the IRA business? Autonomy is essential to the management of an IRA program, primarily because the characteristics of the business are unlike other transaction-dominated services typically offered by banks, and because, as I've stressed before, it is important to maintain one's flexibility in the marketplace. As an example, many institutions make the mistake of trying to fit their IRA programs into their time deposit or brokerage systems. This dependency on unrelated areas not only weakens the priority of the IRA program, but reduces the speed with which needed changes can be made. Also, if one relies on outside parties for services involving direct customer contact, there is always a risk of losing ownership of that customer relationship. Organizationally and strategically, it is best if IRAs can be viewed and evaluated as an independent business encompassing systems, marketing, training, operations, and financial analysis in order to protect the portfolio and to maintain that critical focus on profitability.

Fourth, are you prepared to make the considerable investment in training and marketing that will be required to sell your self-directed program? After all, you may have the most elegant product in the world, but it won't do you any good unless your sales force really understands it and your customers have been made aware of its benefits. Too often this attention to the people side of the IRA business is overlooked because we think it will be too hard to provide staff thorough training and incentive, or because we don't think the customer will know the difference. In order to keep pace with the IRA marketplace, it is essential not to underestimate the abilities of either your employees or your customers, nor the expense required to keep them challenged and motivated.

Finally, consider whether your plans are long range and expandable enough. Any institution, especially a financial institution, takes a long time to make decisions. Make sure that you have built enough time into your planning horizon to accomplish what you really want and to stay ahead of market trends.

8. Case Study: The Union Bank Perspective

Union Bank, headquartered in Los Angeles, California, celebrated its 70th anniversary in 1984 and, in that same year, recorded the highest level of earnings in the bank's history. Another year of record earnings was enjoyed in 1985. Such stability and strength has been achieved by adherence to a philosophy of being "The Business Bank"--primarily a wholesaler of products and services to businesses and other financial institutions rather than a retailer to individuals.

From the bank's emergence in 1914 to its acquisition of trust powers in 1918 to the present, the "Business Bank" strategy has been uppermost in virtually all market planning. This clarity of focus has yielded for the bank a national ranking as number one in correspondent balances from thrift institutions, a well-established niche in the coveted "middle market" and, in the trust area, a dominant market share of the retirement plan (IRA and Keogh[1]) servicing business in the western states.

For more than 20 years, the bank--through its Institutional Trust Services Department--has provided trustee and related operational and technical services to other financial institutions (e.g., savings and loans, banks, and credit unions). At the beginning of 1986, over 540 institutions in seven states were utilizing the bank's specialized products and services in support of IRA and Keogh programs offered to their customers. Union Bank currently acts as trustee for more than 700,000 plans in Alaska, Arizona, California, Florida, Nevada, Oregon and Washington.

The Institutional Trust Services Department is now in the early stages of implementing a program for national expansion. It is expected that its market leadership in the West, the economies of scale inherent in the size of the present customer base, and recently developed technological advances can lead to successful market penetration in other regions of the country.

Another important factor in the department's expected growth is self-directed account (SDA) services which are now widely sought by financial institutions. In this arena, Union Bank has developed yet another

89

specialized service unit known as Market Investment Services Corporation. As a wholly-owned subsidiary of Union Bancorp (the holding company of which Union Bank is the major subsidiary), this organization brings the essential connecting link--investment services--to complete a turn-key package of products and support services which enable a financial institution to offer SDAs to its customers.

Obviously, Institutional Trust Services' growth and success has been due, in large part, to its ability to deliver deposit-generating products and support services to its financial institution customers. That capability and the continuing need for such products will form the basis of the department's future growth, as well.

However, the well-chronicled maturity of the IRA market, accompanied by the accumulation of increasingly significant sums of money by individual account holders, has had an impact on the risk tolerance of a growing segment of the IRA market. Consequently, the traditional fixed-rate, fixed-return certificate of deposit investment for IRAs must, to some extent, give way to investment diversification objectives.

As an IRA account balance reaches $8,000 to $10,000 there is a metamorphosis from IRA savings to IRA investment; in fact, at this writing (early 1986) the low interest rate environment increases the probability that an IRA holder will seek higher yield alternatives.

In other words, the account holder begins to look at investment opportunities beyond CDs. An attitude of capital preservation (risk-averse) shifts to one of capital accumulation (less risk-averse); hence the rise in popularity of the self-directed account (SDA).

Actually, most IRAs and Keoghs are SDAs; the account holders are making their own investment decisions as to institution, rate, term, etc. The exceptions would be those instances where the account holder has employed some other person to make the investment selection. However, in today's retirement plan lexicon, the SDA label is recognized as a reference to a plan or program which gives the account holder access to a broad investment menu (e.g., stocks, bonds, mutual funds, etc.), in addition to the familiar certificate of deposit.

Development of the bank's SDA program actually began in early 1983, well in advance of the current surge of interest. This early start has served to strengthen competitive capability by presenting a tested and seasoned service package.

Ironically, the original SDA concept, which surfaced in the bank's product development area, was very narrow in its scope and did not involve the trust function. Although the majority of the bank's business is with businesses, the initial impetus for SDAs was focused on the individual customer base.

The bank's individual customer base is made up primarily of owners, managers, and executives of existing business relationships. These individuals and their families generally fit the affluent, upscale profile of the

bank's Priority Banking Program target market. Thus, a self-directed
account and related investment services made sense as an offering to that
market. Nevertheless, the bank's existing service relationships with over
500 other financial institutions, each with a segment of its customer base
fitting the SDA target market, presented a potential customer base that would
be several multiples of the Priority Banking Program potential.

In due course, then, the development thrust shifted to the
institutional or wholesale customer base. It should be emphasized,
however, that the Priority Banking customers were not ignored; the scope
was simply broadened to encompass the wholesale approach while also
satisfying the retail market needs. Today, the bank is successfully providing
SDAs to both market segments.

Reference has been made to a turn-key package of products and
services designed to permit a financial institution to offer SDAs to its
customers. At this juncture it may be appropriate to describe the package
and some of its component parts. It may also be useful to explore in some
detail how the program works.

As previously noted, Union Bank utilizes two specialized functional
units to deliver the SDA service--Institutional Trust Services Department and
Market Investment Services Corporation. For ease of reference, the
following discussion will refer to these units as Trust Services and
Investment Services, respectively.

The Trust Services unit can trace its origin back 20 years when it
began providing trustee services for Keogh plans. These services were
being delivered primarily to the savings and loan industry and principally to
members of the California League of Savings Institutions. Even today, both
Trust Services and Investment Services enjoy the endorsement of the
California League and work closely with the League and its members in the
maintenance of qualified plans, refinement of services, and the development
of new products and services.

Trust Services is something of an anomaly in the trust or trustee
industry. In a conventional trust arrangement, assets are held by the trustee
in accordance with the terms of an agreement with the trustor which sets
forth the duties and responsibilities of all parties. The trustee's actions must
be consistent with all applicable laws and regulations, as well as established
fiduciary standards. All of that, except for asset custody, is true in the
structure of services provided by Trust Services.

This important difference arises from the nature of the marketplace
(wholesale) and the target market (other financial institutions). The customer
institutions seek the IRA and Keogh products in order to attract a stable and
growing deposit base; in a conventional trustee arrangement, the deposits
(trust funds) would be with the trustee. In this case, however, the customer
institution acts as Union Bank's agent for holding the trust funds.

Market Investment Services Corporation (Investment Services)
actually came into being in 1984, developed within the bank's funds

management area. This organizational placement of Investment Services gives it the advantage of having the bank's top management on its board of directors. Such a structure also maximizes management commitment to this important enterprise.

Although a young organization, Investment Services and its staff of registered brokers is now handling a trading volume of $6 billion to $7 billion per month. At this time, however, only a small portion of the trading volume relates to SDA transactions. A majority of the activity stems from relationships previously handled elsewhere in the funds management area. Of course, the growing SDA customer base will be easily absorbed into the unit. The high level of trading activity is attributable, in part, to the "Business Bank" orientation of Union Bank and to the multi-faceted nature of Investment Services.

As previously noted, the bank has both retail and wholesale market segments, with emphasis on the latter. This fact has produced three distinct customer strata: individual (largely bank or subsidiary customers), middle market (the bank's business customers), and wholesale (customers of other financial institutions). As noted above, for each of these markets the end product is not only SDA trading; separate, non-retirement plan, trading accounts are also available for individual or company use.

Investment Services' success is also derived from the fact that it offers more than the usual investment services. Beyond providing access to all stock and bond markets, all fixed-income types of investments are accessible (e.g., bankers acceptances, zero coupon bonds, treasury bills, GNMA, etc.). Moreover, four groups of mutual funds are available.

Therefore, from the point of view of a financial institution wishing to introduce an SDA product, Union Bank's Trust Services and Investment Services can combine their specialized capabilities to support the customer institution's needs. In effect, a partnership is created wherein the success of one contributes to the success of all.

Equally important to the institution is recognition that Union Bank's wholesale strategy does not expose its customers to a competing entity. Reinforcing the non-competition aspect, both Trust Services and Investment Services operate in a low-profile, background mode so as not to interject other names between the institution and its customers. For example, when an individual places an investment order by toll-free telephone call, the phone is answered simply "Investment Services," a purposely generic name. Furthermore, the confirmation of the trade sent to the individual bears the name of the financial institution where that person's SDA is held.

Thus, upon execution of separate service agreements with both Trust Services and Investment Services, initial training--from both the trust and brokerage perspectives--is scheduled for the customer institution's personnel. Given the training, any promotional material to be used, and a supply of plan documents, related forms, and brokerage account applications, the institution may begin the sign-up of SDA customers.

93

FIGURE 8.1

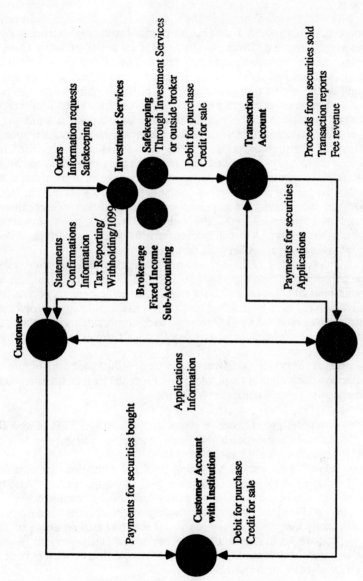

94

Figure 8.1 depicts the typical informational and transactional flows among the institution's customer, the institution itself, and Investment Services.

The "Customer" noted in the diagram is the ultimate end-user, the person establishing the SDA. The "Financial Institution" is Union Bank's (Investment Services) customer. Two accounts are shown--the Customer Account with Institution and the Transaction Account. The former represents the individual's SDA; the latter a correspondent, clearing account through which transaction settlements are effected. An identical structure would, of course, apply for a non-SDA arrangement; however, the Customer Account would be separate from the same individual's SDA.

With Investment Services filling the broker role, there is no need for the financial institution to have registered brokers on staff. The institution's customer contact personnel need only serve in a customer relations capacity, providing information and account applications. The customer forwards the completed application directly to Investment Services who will, in turn, advise the individual of acceptance of the application. Thereafter, for investment transactions only, the individual calls a toll-free telephone number which provides direct access, from 6:00 a.m. to 3:00 p.m. Pacific time, with the Investment Services brokers.

Investment Services applies discounted commission rates to each stock or corporate bond transaction initiated by an individual; the total commission is incorporated into the transaction settlement. A portion of the commission revenue is shared with the financial institutions, based on the commissions generated by their respective customers. This revenue sharing is in exchange for the initial customer contact duties performed by the institutions' personnel.

Trust Services' involvement is not illustrated in Figure 8.1; nonetheless, the unit plays a pivotal role. From the trust or fiduciary side of the house, so to speak, comes the following:

•**Plan Design.** Master or prototype plans (IRA, SEP, Keogh [both defined contribution and defined benefit], etc.) have been developed for each type of financial institution.
•**Plan Maintenance.** Changing laws and regulations are continually monitored to ensure compliance and IRS qualification. Assistance can also be provided for plans developed by other sources.
•**Plan Trustee.** Applicable fiduciary responsibilities are assumed. If desired, a non-fiduciary, custodial role can also be arranged. Plan transfers and distributions are monitored and approved. A verbal authorization process is available to avoid delays often experienced with mail turnaround time.

All required reporting (1099-R, W-2P, 5498, etc.) is generated to plan participants and the appropriate government agencies.

•**Advisory Services.** Qualified retirement plan specialists are available on toll-free telephones to assist with technical and administrative questions and to help resolve complex issues that may arise, such as attachments, tax levies, divorce decrees, bankruptcy claims, and other legal processes. Whenever appropriate, the advisory staff works in conjunction with the customer institution's local counsel.

•**Training.** Employees of customer institutions are given comprehensive training, both at inception and periodically throughout the year. The training goal is to provide institution personnel with the knowledge required to sell effectively and administer retirement plan products.

When the service relationship includes a trade organization, such as a savings and loan league, assistance can be provided in developing and presenting league-sponsored workshops.

As a special marketing tool, the training specialists can also conduct accredited and non-accredited programs for specific customer groups of an institution (e.g., CPAs, attorneys, etc.).

•**Marketing.** In some cases generic marketing materials (brochures, statement stuffers, newspaper ads, etc.) are available. Assistance can also be provided for the development of customized items.

•**Technical Information.** A topical newsletter, *ITS Viewpoint*, is published periodically, along with administrative and operational bulletins, to keep the institutions' staffs abreast of legal, regulatory, technical, and procedural issues.

•**Documents and Forms.** All plan documents and related forms and all transactional forms (distributions, transfers, etc.) have been designed and can be supplied in specified quantities.

•**Participation.** Trust Services can participate in trade group activities through regularly scheduled meetings, committee groups, etc., to ensure communication and coordination among the group, its members, and the assigned retirement plan specialists.

With the combined resources of Union Bank's Trust Services and Investment Services, a financial institution can achieve easy entry into the retirement plan business both conventional and SDA. Or if an institution is already offering retirement plans to its customers, the bank's services can help simplify the administrative and operational burdens of their existing programs. From the institution's point of view, it becomes a "make or buy" decision. In other words, either attempt to duplicate all the capabilities enumerated in the foregoing or utilize an outside service provider.

The bank's 20 years of retirement plan service experience have seen the passage of many interesting points along the learning curve. The birth of

ERISA in 1974, IRA the next year, universal IRA in 1982, and TEFRA, DEFRA, and REA in quick succession, have all provided both challenges and opportunities.

In the early years, the business was paper-driven and labor-intensive. To some extent, this is still true; the legal nature of retirement plan documents and the exacting requirements of applicable regulations make it so. Nevertheless, the sheer magnitude of today's book of business and the coast-to-coast span of existing relationships demands efficient, responsive, and flexible data processing capabilities. Therefore, as much as possible, paper must be immobilized or, at the very least, removed from time-critical transactions. To this end, Trust Services' processing system has been developed internally and has evolved to a real-time, on-line system with processing capabilities within the customer's office by use of remote terminals.

Today, Trust Services and its partner, Investment Services, have the capability and unrestrained capacity to serve a still growing, albeit at a slower rate, market. Also, the technology now available can effectively support and be responsive to the changing retirement plans environment. Best of all, the efficient use of automation and high caliber personnel has resulted in a very cost-efficient service delivery which translates into competitive products and services for the IRA and Keogh marketplace.

Before closing, a few comments on the IRA and SDA markets seem appropriate. The opportunity to deal with hundreds of financial institutions and hundreds of thousands of their customers, has given rise to several perceptions with significant marketing implications. Briefly, the comments are as follows:

SEASONALITY

In a very predictable cycle, IRA advertising and promotion seems to surface in January and submerge after April 15 of each year. Over the remainder of the year, the general public hears or sees very little on the subject. And, in fact, available statistics reveal that 80 percent of annual IRA contributions are made during the first 3-1/2 months of the year and most are for the prior tax year.

However, the growth in numbers of accounts has led to dispersion of CD maturities throughout the year. This creates a reinvestment market well outside the 3-1/2 month marketing window and, with low interest rates, institutions are vulnerable to the loss of relationships if they have no SDA product. Even in a healthier interest rate climate, the vulnerability remains high if no marketing outreach effort is expended.

Beyond the dispersion of maturities, another factor making IRAs a year-round market relates to the public's increasing tendency to shift investments to different vehicles whenever the current choice does not meet expectations. This is, of course, a by-product of the SDA market itself. The mobility of the work force and the portability (rollover) of vested retirement plan benefits have also broadened the IRA season.

THE "$2,000 MINDSET"

It is well-documented that public participation in IRAs is skewed to the higher income levels. There is an obvious correlation with disposable income; however, a contributing factor may be the general tenor of most advertising and promotion. Emphasis or prominent mention, is usually given to the $2,000 maximum for each employed person. Consequently, there may be a large segment of the public that believes they must have $2,000 in hand in order to have an IRA.

A corollary cause may be the lack of promotion for IRA contributions by payroll deduction. It would seem that credit unions in particular have an advantage in this regard, which should be further exploited.

DISINTERMEDIATION

This lofty sounding word simply reflects a common fear of many institutions considering SDAs, that is, that use of the product will stimulate outflow of deposits. It is generally believed, however, that this process has already occurred. Therefore, rather than avoiding the process, hesitant institutions may be prolonging it for lack of having the product available.

Furthermore, an added product (SDA) can help to solidify existing relationships and retain some of the individual's deposits, and avoid the loss of both the relationship and all the deposits. In fact, there can often be an inflow of deposits when an individual consolidates multiple service needs within the institution which can serve all those needs.

SDA RETAIL MARKETING STRATEGY

Many institutions who have implemented an SDA product are indicating the intent to utilize a defensive marketing strategy: minimal promotion but ready presentation of the product when a customer inquires about it. This approach is used where the aforementioned disintermediation concerns are strong.

Union Bank's Trust and Investment Services units now have more than 50 institutions using the SDA product. Experience clearly reveals that those adopting an active advertising and promotional campaign have achieved significant success, and disintermediation, if any, is more than offset by commission revenue sharing. Without exception, the active institutions are very pleased with the SDA's positive impact on their customers.

WHOLESALE MARKETING STRATEGY

The bank's close association with the California League of Savings Institutions and the collaboration between the league, its members, and the bank has proven beneficial to all parties. Moreover, this relationship serves as a model for Trust Services' national expansion marketing strategy. The intent is to win acceptance or endorsements from similar financial institution trade groups, thereby, gaining the groups' assistance in promoting the products and services to its members. Such an approach will be far more effective and less costly than a one-on-one sales campaign especially in areas of the country where the bank is not yet well known.

As service providers to IRA, Keogh, and self-directed account retailers, the success of both Trust Services and Investment Services is, in large part, dependent on the success of their institutional customers. Accordingly, as future changes occur in the retirement plan area, another marketing strategy is to be responsive to the changes; a hard-won market share can be easily lost if "high tech" is permitted to supplant "high touch." The compelling need for automated processes to accommodate high volume activities and the essential electronic links to span large geographic distances and multiple time zones cannot reduce the importance of personal contact and communication.

The value of personal contact and communication is, of course, one of the fundamental truths. However, in an industry subject to many internal and external forces for change and many such changes subject to interpretation, the fundamentals cannot be overlooked. Regulatory changes, new products and services, new competition, and, in a macro sense, changes in the nation's economy and its financial and investment markets can all have profound impacts on the IRA market. In turn, with the IRA portfolio at $225 billion and rising, impacts on the IRA market will cause measurable changes in many related areas.

What better reason, then, for personal contact and communication? The IRA market is already a very important industry; the SDA market is sure to be an important segment of it. Those who will succeed will be those who listen and respond to their current and prospective customers' needs. Furthermore, as service providers, the communication process should be two way to effect a true partnership of ideas and resources leading to mutual success.

NOTES

[1]Throughout this chapter the term "Keogh" will appear; this is done simply for ease of reference. The Tax Equity and Fiscal Responsibility Act (TEFRA) removed virtually all distinctions between a retirement plan for self-

employed individuals (Keogh) and such a plan for incorporated businesses. Accordingly, a corporate plan may be used by the self-employed; consequently, the term "Keogh" is falling into disuse.

In different parts of the country, different terminology has sprung up to describe what used to be a Keogh plan. In Florida, "Parity Plan" is the operative term; in California it's "Defined Contribution Plan" or "Basic Retirement Plan." Other variations have been heard in other regions. The reader might consider this note a challenge to develop a new, generic term that could receive wide acceptance and use in our industry.

9. Case Study: ISFA Corporation

By the year 1990, IRA assets are estimated to exceed $500 billion, making them second only to pension funds as a block of savings dollars.[1] Are banks and thrifts positioned to capture effectively a large portion of these assets?

Banks and thrifts are already major players in the insured direct IRA market. But is it important for depository institutions to enter the self-directed market?

Recent research studies by Kenneth C. Kehrer Associates[2] and others show conclusively that the fastest growing segment of the IRA market is self-directed. Table 9.1 shows the growth in IRA assets by type of account. Customer demographic studies also clearly point to the importance of the self-directed market in terms of long-term customer relationships and the development of the one-stop financial service entity. A recent report in the *Wall Street Journal*[3] cited an 80 percent jump in mutual fund sales in IRAs from 1984 to 1985, twice the rate for insured deposits. IRA balances in excess of $10,000 have now surpassed 30 percent of those U.S. households that have established IRAs, and recent research shows these IRA owners have moved all or part of their accounts at some time.

TABLE 9.1
IRA ASSETS BY TYPE OF ACCOUNT

	Total	Self-Directed		Commercial Banks		Savings Institutions		Other	
	$B	$B	%	$B	%	$B	%	$B	%
Dec 31 '81	26	0.5	2	7	28	12	48	6	22
Dec 31 '83	92	7	8	27	29	32	35	26	28
Dec 31 '84	132	15	11	37	28	43	33	37	28
Dec 31 '85	196	26	14	52	26	57	29	61	31

This research has not gone unnoticed by other financial institutions. Indeed, brokerage firms, insurance companies, and others are now aggressively trying to attract insured IRA customers with higher yielding and more flexible investment alternatives.[4] Clearly, in order to retain assets and remain competitive, depository institutions must aggressively enter the self-directed market.

But there are other reasons to enter this arena:

- Potential for significant fee income
- Strengthened customer relationships
- Developing new customer relationships
- Effectively establishing a position in the financial services market

Once banks, thrifts, and credit unions decide to make self-directed IRAs available, two key questions must be addressed: How should this market be entered and what products should be sold? I specifically use the word *sold* and not offered, since banks and thrifts that have merely offered other non-traditional products and services (like discount brokerages) have, by and large, been unsuccessful.

Depository institutions have several choices as to how to enter this market. Among them are purchasing a broker-dealer, filing with the SEC under Rule 3b-9 and forming a broker-dealer, or participating in a joint venture program with an organization such as the ISFA Group that offers the INVEST service. ISFA, a full-service investment firm, began operations in late 1982. It is predominantly owned by 32 depository institutions in key markets across the country. Currently, there are 170 banks and thrifts subscribing to the service, representing over 250 operating INVEST offices and 1,000 NASD Series 7 licensed brokers. In addition to its INVEST service, the ISFA Group also offers the INSURE program to banks and thrifts for insurance products, and ISFA Mortgage Funding is an issuer of collateralized mortgage obligations.

Although INVEST has been in operation for over three years, our self-directed IRA program began in 1984, and 1985 was its first full year of existence. Our 1985 self-directed business totaled approximately 12,000 retail accounts, representing approximately $85 million. This translates into $7,100 per account. This high balance indicates the success we've had selling to the rollover market.

Table 9.2 shows an approximate breakdown of INVEST's IRA business by product category, commissions charged on these products, and how these are shared with INVEST subscribers (before potential payment of bonus revenue available under ISFA's bonus schedule).

TABLE 9.2
INVEST Subscriber IRA Product Sales & Payouts

Product	Typical Commission	Percent To INVEST Subscriber	Percent of Product IRA Type in All INVEST Accounts
Mutual Funds	4%-8%	65%	55%
U.S. Gov't.			
Other Bond Funds			
Equity Funds			
Real Estate Limited Partnerships	8%	65%	10%
Zero Coupon Bonds	1%-3%	65%	10%
Equities	1%-4%	50%	15%
Bonds	1/2%-3%	50%	3%
Other	1/4%-8%	50%-60%	7%

It's apparent that the products customers want are the packaged types of investments such as mutual funds, unit investment trusts, and limited partnerships. Our sales of mutual funds have been concentrated in the U.S. Government and "Ginnie Mae" types. These funds have an average of approximately 4 percent sales load with 65 percent paid to the subscriber. This equals $184 net revenue per IRA account to the subscribing bank or thrift. There also may be significant additional revenue generated as customers change their holdings and additional purchases are made.

These products have been sold by INVEST subscribers primarily utilizing four different marketing strategies:

- Advertising
- Direct mail
- Public seminars
- Internal marketing

While the first three methods are frequently used, many institutions overlook internal programs that should be used to complement and enhance the other marketing strategies. These internal programs include:

- Prominent lobby signage
- Employee awareness programs
- Referral and incentive programs
- Cross-selling training
- Customer awareness campaigns
- Telemarketing
- Person-to-person selling

The INVEST subscribers cited in the two case studies that follow utilized both public advertising and, to some extent, internal support programs. (These two institutions requested to remain anonymous and, also at their request, reprints of their advertisements are not available).

Savings and Loan A is located in a major southern metropolitan area and was one of the earliest INVEST subscribers. Asset size is approximately $1.5 billion in 29 branches and 10 INVEST centers. The institution ran a half-page, generic advertisement in its city's two major newspapers. Running twice weekly during March 1985, the ads showed a "thin man" and a "fat man" and had the headline: "If Your Bank's IRA Options are a Little Thin, Open Your IRA at A." The ad, however, was not effectively supported by a systematic or organized internal marketing program. With only a telephone number to call for additional information, the ad resulted in little or no direct business. The generic nature of the ad was later determined to be one cause of the poor results generated. In addition, it was felt that the March insertions were too late for the 1984 IRA season. These facts combined to cause the ad program to bring disappointing results.

Savings Bank B, located in New England, also used public advertising to promote self-directed IRA business. Its ad focused on a lapel button with a large "Me" and used the heading: "The Only Real Interest is Self Interest." This ad, placed in two dailies and three weeklies, was run weekly in February, the last two weeks in March, and the first two weeks in April. Supporting this ad, the institution also conducted radio advertising, as well as employee training and incentive programs. By conducting customer interviews, it was determined that 51 new self-directed IRA accounts were opened in direct response to the ad, and that 31 of these (61 percent) were new to the bank. It was further determined that these accounts brought in approximately $200,000 in new funds to the bank.

Subscribers to the INVEST program have significant flexibility to use the types of marketing and advertising that best meet the needs of their target markets. With this in mind, INVEST, working with its key product providers such as Kemper Financial Services, Franklin Funds, JMB Realty Corporation, and John Nuveen & Company, make available a wide range of customized marketing materials. Our research has shown that the prominent display of an interest rate or return or product-specific marketing materials is very effective.

Recently, INVEST subscribers have begun to use direct mail pieces and statement stuffers, all provided at no cost, that focus on the yield or return of the product combined with some type of features and benefits presentation. Usually designed with a response card for further information, the effectiveness of these types of marketing programs, in conjunction with internal marketing support, has been well documented.

Failure of these types of programs can usually be traced to senior management's fear of "cannibalizing" core CD deposits. In fact, the entire disintermediation issue must be resolved prior to offering any new non-traditional product. Management must come to grips with the fact that today's consumers are more knowledgeable. The media is bombarding them with many attractive investment alternatives. The future of banks and thrifts lies in selling quality financial products of all kinds, extending customer relationships, and establishing new sources of fee income.

To be successful in marketing self-directed IRAs or any new product or service, depository institutions must determine their:

- Goals
- Market
- Customer demographics
- Product expertise

And regardless of the specific marketing strategy utilized, there are five keys to success:

- Careful and thorough preparation
- Intelligent product selection
- Internal support
- Good timing
- Thorough follow-up

In conclusion, one must be mindful that the competition is mounting an all-out battle to establish firmly its dominance in the self-directed IRA marketplace. Right now, your customers are being exposed to sophisticated investment choices from national and regional brokerage firms, insurance companies, and other depository institutions. The winners in this war will be the full-service financial services organizations that enthusiastically and aggressively meet the needs of today's and tomorrow's consumers.

NOTES

[1]Edwin A. Finn, Jr. and Dan Baum, "IRA Assets Second Only to Pension Funds," *Wall Street Journal,* January, 1985.
[2]Kenneth Kehrer, *The Ira Market: Growing Opportunities for the Financial Services Industry,* Kenneth Kehrer Associates, Princeton, N.J., November, 1985.
[3]"Brokers Seen Consolidating Gains in IRAs This Year," *Wall Street Letter,* January, 1986.
[4]*Ibid.*

Trust Administration

Critical to offering a successful self-directed IRA is the ability to provide sufficiently flexible trust administration to accommodate the wide range of consumer choice the product potentially can provide. The administrative services required from a trustee will include recordkeeping, account valuation, IRS reporting, compliance review, billing, asset valuation, and client communication. Given the complexity of the self-directed IRA, performing these services will require relatively sophisticated computer capability and software development.

Still, professional trust administration is required if all relevant regulations are to be met and the account is to remain tax-qualified. So, too, will ultimate customer satisfaction depend upon the ability of the trustee to provide complete, accurate, and timely information at a competitive cost. The trustee then must interface among many players: the broker selling the account and placing subsequent orders; the exchange, investment company, insurance carrier, or depository institution providing the product; the regulatory agencies, including the IRS, demanding contribution and distribution reports; and the client who may, from time to time, want almost instantaneous account valuation and will demand regular, periodic, comprehensive, consolidated reports detailing all transaction activity, listing fees, and accurately valuing assets.

The foundation of professional trust administration should not be underestimated, because it is frequently the fulcrum upon which the whole system rests for support and continuance.

Mary Mohr does an excellent job of specifying decision criteria for selecting a trustee. Those institutions seeking to develop their own trust capabilities can read Ms. Mohr's chapter with a view toward identifying those abilities they themselves must develop to be competitive. While the competitors of First Trust may have ranked themselves somewhat differently had they constructed Ms. Mohr's analytic matrices, Mohr is to be complimented for providing competitor locational information so readers can check for themselves.

10. Self-Directed IRAs: Trust Administration Requirements

Trust administration for self-directed IRAs can be a complicated subject to understand and a difficult job to do for several reasons. There are multiple legal arenas which impact this field, including federal IRS Code law, federal securities law, state banking law, and state securities law. When you add these often conflicting, if not confusing, laws and guidelines, their interplay on the day-to-day administration of an individual retirement account, and then multiply these problems geometrically by the volume of accounts in various states, you perceive some notion of the challenge of trust administration today. The purpose of this chapter is to provide a better understanding of trust administration, so that you and your firm can make a sound business decision as to whether or not you should enter this business and the best way to do so. If you decide to enter this market, you then must decide whether to "grow your own" trust administration department, through internal organizational development, or to buy these services from an outside purveyor, such as an independent trust company.

At this point, you may feel somewhat like the late Israeli leader, Dr. Weizmann, who once sailed to America with Albert Einstein on a Zionist mission. When they arrived in New York City, Dr. Weizmann was asked how he and the great scientist interacted. He replied, "Well, throughout the voyage Professor Einstein kept talking about *his* theory of relativity," When Weizmann was asked his opinion about this subject, he said, "It seems to me that *he* understands it very well!"

Although you may have been hesitant until now to delve into self-direction due to its more technical administrative aspects and potential liabilities, the subject is not overwhelming. It is a natural business extension of the cash-based IRA administration you are doing.

Among the issues to be discussed are what criteria you should use when selecting a trustee and what special reporting and accounting requirements are created by self-direction. In addition, we will look at the major companies currently offering self-directed administration and the price of their services, and we will determine how to evaluate the costs/benefits of the services provided.[1]

SELECTING A TRUSTEE

Track Record

What criteria should you use when selecting a trustee? First, consider the track record of the trustee, that is, its business reputation and longevity in the self-directed market. Also, identify the trustee's historical business roots (i.e., banking or brokerage). Talk to the personnel in marketing, compliance, and operations to evaluate their levels of expertise, their degrees of knowledge and breadth, and how well they work as an integrated team. Decide for yourself how flexible they and their trust administration firm appear to be. Ask questions about your unique problems to learn whether the personnel have tackled them before. When conducting your due diligence search for a trustee, your goal is to find people *compatible* with your needs and business objectives. If you can buy this expertise and ability to work together cooperatively, you may save time and money when catapulting your organization into the self-directed marketplace.

For example, our firm, First Trust Corporation of Denver, Colorado, has been in the self-directed administration business since 1962 when it pioneered a self-directed Keogh prototype. (A prototype is a pre-approved plan that is in compliance with IRS law.) Our business roots are grounded in brokerage; we serve more than 20,000 registered representatives in all 50 states. Currently, First Trust Corporation administers 135,000 retirement plans and holds more than $990 million in assets.

When it comes to selecting a trustee, remember the adage which tells us that you can't be all things to all people. What you are looking for in a trustee is expertise and experience in very specific areas.

Necessary Services

The second major criterion you should use in selecting a trustee is to determine whether or not the trustee can provide at least the more important administrative services you will need. You should ask questions about the computer hardware capacity, software development, and, critically important in this area, the ability to grow with the ever-changing legislative demands. Due to the rapid growth of and interest in the self-directed market, large and small firms are struggling to keep up with the increase in computer demands. Understand the unusual blend of programming skills needed to take IRS Code rules and regulations and convert them to financial asset tracking and valuation reporting. These skills take time to develop, and the expertise is not always readily available.

Does the trustee have the ability to provide private label services for your firm? Private labels typically require customized printing of documents and sales materials, special account coding, billing and fee collection, and restrictions on the types of investments allowed in the accounts. For example, many thrift institutions entering this market are allowing only selected mutual funds and limited partnerships in their private label IRAs. Will the trustee provide you with what you need while giving you the flexibility to add investment alternatives in the future? Your institution will need to determine which investments make sense for your client base, are most profitable for your firm, and minimize your liability. Be sure to find a trustee with the capacity to handle more complex investments than you currently may need to ensure your ability to add new products in the future.

When selecting a trustee you also are shopping for the ability to access answers to technical compliance questions. Interview members of the compliance staff for in-house levels of expertise, and find out which outside law firms are used by the trustee. One difficulty in finding correct answers to legal questions is the multiple arenas of law discussed earlier. You may think you are asking a straightforward ERISA question when, in fact, there are significant SEC or state banking law implications lurking in the ether as unraised issues. The experienced compliance officer, in conjunction with a coordinated effort from outside counsel, must be able to give you a more developed answer to complicated and often uncharted legal areas.

Perhaps the most important service/benefit you buy when you select a trustee is communication. You not only need to investigate the initial communications tools to be used between your firm and the trustee, you also must evaluate the ongoing communication links. Can you, your staff, and your clients access current account data via toll-free lines? Is the management of client services structured to maximize telephone access? Test market the trustees by asking them questions such as these: How do I set up a contributory rollover account? How do I handle a mutual fund transaction? How do dividends get added to my IRA? Also, be aware of the levels of courtesy, patience, efficiency, and follow-up exhibited by the service personnel. Their attitudes toward you will reflect how your clients will be handled.

As one of my favorite American authors, Mark Twain, once noted, "To be understood is a luxury." However, when you are choosing a trustee, the company's ability to understand and work with you is an absolute necessity.

From a more tangible perspective, you will need to ascertain the frequency and degree of detail of the account statements. The statement is the primary "product" the trustee generates for you and your clients. Is it legible, simple to understand, complete (with explanation codes), accurate, and timely? The true test of an administration firm lies in the evaluation of these features of its consolidated statements. The statement should reflect each asset, all transactions, the number of shares/units held, the current value of each holding, any dividends/interest, and the cash balances.

Other types of tangible communications also may be provided by the trustee. Your institution may or may not want these communications to be sent directly to your clients. For example, an annual/quarterly newsletter may accompany each statement. Can the trustee customize this newsletter to make its image consistent with that of your institution's image? Also, ask to see copies of such client correspondence as a "request for distribution" form.

Recordkeeping and Accounting

The next major concern to be addressed is the special recordkeeping and accounting requirements created by self-direction. Your trustee must report to various government agencies, participants must report to government agencies, and the trustee must report to the participants and their beneficiaries. Self-directed administration can be viewed in terms of who has to report what to whom, when they must do so, and what happens if they don't report accurately and promptly.

The key enforcing agency for IRAs is the Internal Revenue Service (IRS). The IRS expects reports when taxable events or incidents of taxation occur. The trustee, for example, must report all IRA contributions and the tax year for which they are intended on Form 5498. The 5498 report also includes information regarding the amount of rollover contributions vs. regular IRA contributions, so the trustee must have the sophisticated data processing capability to keep track of such information. The 5498 form must be furnished to participants and to the IRS by May 31 of the following calendar year and must reflect contributions made through April 15 of that year. In addition, the trustee must report all distributions made during the calendar year. For any periodic or partial distributions Form W-2P is used, and Form 1099R is used for total distribution. The withholding of federal income tax must be made for all distributions unless the participant specifies otherwise. If the trustee fails to report any IRA contribution, the penalty is $50 per account. Therefore, liability for the trustee is a substantial business risk because the trustee's annual revenue per account probably is less than $50. For distributions, the penalty would be $50 per incident in the event that there was improper reporting of distributions or if the 1099R or W-2P was not generated promptly.

What must the participant report to the IRS? The participant is going to report the deduction on his 1040. Distributions would be reported on the participant's 1040 as annual income.

The Trust Agreement

What does the trustee have to report to the participants and beneficiaries? The IRS requires IRA trustees to furnish certain information to the individual on whose behalf the accounts are maintained. The IRS regulations spell out in some detail what the trustee is required to report. For example, the trustee must furnish a copy of the trust agreement and the disclosure statement at least seven (7) days before the IRA is established or no later than the day of establishment, if the individual is permitted to revoke the IRA. Internal Revenue Code Section 408(i) requires the trustee to furnish disclosure statements to "benefitted individuals." A benefitted individual is one for whom the IRA will be established. These disclosure statements are supposed to be the plain English version of the trust agreement. They must be provided along with the actual trust agreement at or before the time the account is established. If the disclosure statement or trust agreement ever is amended, which recently has been occurring rather regularly, that amendment also must be provided to the participants. The trustee also must report all distributions from the plan to participants, with a copy of the W-2P or 1099R, and all contributions to the plan on Form 5498 to the participant.

What should you look for in the provisions of a trust agreement? First, the document must be in compliance with current Code law. It should be drafted broadly to allow maximum flexibility in investment alternatives, even though your institution may not perceive an immediate need for a full spectrum of investments. You can limit your acceptable investments by publishing a currently acceptable range of investment options. In addition, look at the time requirements for giving notice to customers of changes in the plan document, procedures, fees, etc. The trust document needs to be a working contract that can be administered efficiently on a daily basis. One of the key benefits you purchase with a prototype trust document is that the trustee updates the plan and there usually is no charge to your firm or the clients. Contrast this with drafting and maintaining your own prototype, which requires a high degree of legal expertise as well as establishing an ongoing relationship with counsel who must follow all current legislation to keep your plan in compliance.

TRUSTEE RESPONSIBILITIES

The Annual Report

The trustee also usually sends an annual report which accurately discloses the value of the account at the end of the calendar year, which may be compiled on the fourth quarter's statement.

The valuation process is a timely and expensive one for the trustee. Depending on the complexity of assets held in the accounts, the process can be relatively simple or very convoluted. For example, if limited partnerships are held, how are they valued at the end of the trustee's valuation period? Usually the trustee reports only that information currently supplied by the product sponsor or issuer. What if the trustee receives no information from the issuer? Typically, the trustee will fall back to the purchase amount to set a current valuation on the asset. These hard-to-value assets make the accounting function very cumbersome. When selecting a trustee, you may want to find out how and when assets are valued.

Penalties

What penalties are triggered if the trustee fails to furnish the disclosure statement, a trust agreement, or any amendments to the trust agreement? There can be a $50 IRS penalty for each violation, depending on the facts and circumstances of each situation.

Distributions

One of the key issues in plan administration today is recordkeeping for distributions. The industry now is seeing an increased demand for a firm's distribution policy to be flexible and to suit the individual customer's needs. No doubt, this trend will continue to escalate. On the one hand the IRS rules governing the requirements will become more complex as more IRA participants come of age for distributions. Yet the participants will expect ease of withdrawal analogous to checking accounts and ATMs. Legislative changes in this area will more than likely continue their meanderings, making life difficult for programmers and compliance officers who must attempt to interpret these changing laws and regulations. Penalties for early withdrawals by participants from their IRAs currently are not assessed in the event of death, disability, or distributions after age 59-1/2. If early withdrawals are taken, a 10 percent tax is assessed on the amount withdrawn, but the new tax law may change this to 20 percent (or 15 percent, depending upon which version passes).

Shared Reporting

Another growing challenge is shared trustee reporting among institutions that concurrently provide different trustee functions to the same individual. For example, a local thrift institution offers a certificate of deposit IRA. It also offers a self-directed IRA. In January of 1986, it accepts a 1985 contribution on behalf of the participant in a CD IRA. In February of 1986, the participant opens a self-directed IRA with a national trust company and makes a $2,000 1986 contribution. Then, in March 1986, the participant decides to consolidate his IRAs and transfers the CD IRA to the self-directed IRA. Who must report what? The thrift institution must report the 1985 contribution on Form 5498; the national trust company must report the 1986 contribution on Form 5498; and no reporting is required for the trustee to trustee transfer. Once the transfer is completed, the successor trustee will have full reporting requirements including distributions.

THE ADVANTAGES OF SELF-DIRECTION AND INDEPENDENT TRUSTEES

In summary, there are numerous reasons why the thrift institution should expand its products to include self-direction. First, thrifts are losing their market share to competitors in the brokerage and banking industries who are offering more sophisticated customers more flexible, higher return products. Second, the costs of building and maintaining an internal operations center to handle complex administrative functions usually exceed revenues, leaving marginal profits at best. And, most importantly, conversion of demand deposit dollars to security and insurance products generates commissions. The potential profit margin on security and insurance products far exceeds the current spread thrifts can generate on cash products. In short, if thrifts are looking ahead, they will see a sustained if not growing market share, a reduction in cost centers, and the increased profitability in commissions that can be achieved by instituting a self-directed IRA program and utilizing the services of an independent trust company.

Trustees: How to Evaluate Fees and Services

When shopping for a trustee to handle your firm's self-directed IRAs, look for complete menus of services and products at comparable fees/prices.

The cost of changing trustees can be significant from the standpoint of reputation as well as time and dollars; therefore, the following factors should be viewed as important elements when evaluating the overall mix of services offered by any trustee.

Remember that you are in the "consumer" role at this point, and don't allow technical jargon and multitudes of figures to confuse you. It is easy to feel the strain put upon us by our own technological advances, but one also can learn to laugh about the problem. As the saying goes, "The computer didn't eliminate red tape; it only perforated it."

New Account Fees. These generally range up to $25.00 per account; there also may be a transfer-in fee for each existing IRA transferred to the successor trustee. If your firm has a large volume of existing IRAs with cash and CDs only, you may shop for trustees that will waive establishment fees on a bulk transfer.

Annual Fees. Trustees charge in one of three ways: a flat or fixed annual administration fee, a variable asset fee based on the current value of the account, or a transaction fee based on the number and type of trading activities in the account. Trustees also may have some combination of these fees such as a $25 annual administration fee plus a $15 per transaction fee.

The type and frequency of trading you expect your client base to conduct should be a key factor in selecting a trustee; the company should have a fee schedule that suits *your* needs. If you anticipate a high volume of large rollover accounts or IRAs that will trade frequently, consider trustees who offer an asset-based fee so your clients will not be assessed both a transaction fee and a commission every time a trade is made. A typical asset-based fee schedule will begin at 1 percent and scale down as the asset value increases, usually averaging between .25 percent and .5 percent.

Transaction Fees. These fees are charged for the purchase and sale of stocks, bonds, mutual funds, limited partnerships, etc. Different fees may be charged based on the type of investment traded. Check to see what triggers a fee; for example, will posting a dividend activate an additional fee? Will a per-check fee be charged for each distribution check? There should be *no* fees for cash or money market transactions.

Termination Fees. Most trustees charge termination fees for accounts that transfer out to other trustees or terminate by taking a total distribution. Some charge, even if the participant terminates due to death, disability, or retirement. These fees usually are in a 1 percent of asset value range or are a set amount. Consider asking for a ceiling on termination fees as a negotiating chip with a trustee.

Other Fees. Read the fine print to determine the circumstances under which the trustee can charge additional fees for "extraordinary services." Will researching old account information and statements to resolve a disputed dividend cost the client so much per statement?

COMPARING TRUSTEES

Statement Frequency

Most trustees have the ability to generate statements quarterly. You may or may not need more than an annual statement, depending on the frequency of other communications generated by the brokerage firm or product sponsor. Typically, the last calendar quarter statement serves as an annual statement, even though it may not be cumulative for the tax year.

Fee Collection and Billing

The statement usually doubles as a fee collection device so the trustee can pay itself. Find out the details of this process. Are all accounts with positive cash balances "swept" so the trustee can pay itself? What procedures will the trustee implement to liquidate assets to pay its fees?

Cash Handling

Most trustees provide several cash options including FDIC insured passbook accounts as well as money market funds. Ascertain whether there is a minimum balance for the money market sweeps.

Acceptable Investments

The general guidelines a trustee must follow when accepting investments are set by the IRS, such as the rules which disallow hard assets and whole life insurance. Other guidelines are set by the trustee based on what they can efficiently administer; for example, a trustee might not permit margin accounts and short sales. Furthermore, some investments may be costly to administer (e.g., second trust deeds and real estate), so the trustee may disallow them even though they are allowed by the IRS.

Other Services

Additional services that more effectively facilitate communications also should be considered. For example, sufficient numbers of incoming (and outgoing) toll-free lines, with enough trained personnel staffing them, are essential to communications. A trustee newsletter also may be available. Ask what support is provided for researching and answering client questions. Determine what training is available for your staff on both a start-up and ongoing basis.

National Trustees. The following firms currently are offering self-directed IRA administration services. Call them for current fee information:

First Trust Corporation
Denver, Colorado
303-744-2944
800-525-2124 (New Plans)
800-525-8188 (Existing Plans)

State Street Bank & Trust Co.
Boston, Massachusetts
617-786-3000

Plymouth Home National Bank
Brockton, Massachusetts
617-583-6700

Bank of Beverly Hills
Glendale, California
818-246-8330

118

Trust Company of America
Boulder, Colorado
303-449-3300

Lincoln Trust
Denver, Colorado
303-771-1900

California Federal Savings and Loan
Los Angeles, California
213-932-2200
800-922-3539

Richfield Bank & Trust
Richfield, Minnesota
612-861-7355

Delaware Charter Guarantee and Trust Co.
Wilmington, Delaware
302-995-2131

Retirement Accounts, Inc.
Winter Park, Florida
305-644-2002
800-325-4352

The following firms also provide turn-key trustee services:

First Trust Corporation
Denver, Colorado
303-744-2944
800-525-2124 (New Plans)
800-525-8188 (Existing Plans)

Provident National Bank
Philadelphia, Pennsylvania
800-523-1526

Bank of San Diego
San Diego, California
619-237-5300

The Competitive Map

One marketing tool used to categorize key benefits of a product or brand is a brand map or matrix. This map has two axes which delineate benefits. In this case, the vertical axis is service with a high, active degree of trustee service at the top and a more passive degree of service at the bottom. See Figure 10.1. Along the horizontal axis is price, with low prices at the left and high prices at the right. This competitive map is derived by applying the following case: A new IRA is established January 1, 1984. Contributions of $2,000 are made in order to purchase a publicly-traded stock. The plan is then terminated as of December 31, 1984.

This competitive map may be a useful tool for evaluating the fees for services provided by numerous trustees. However, this area is riddled with difficulty, because not all trustees charge fees in the same way for the same services. Be sure you are comparing apples with apples, or you will get lost in the maze of technical definitions of similar services using different names.

FIGURE 10.1
Competitive Map of Major Trustees
Administering Self-Directed IRAs

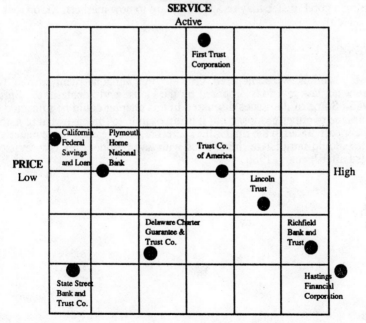

120

CONCLUSION

You are encouraged to look for full service, excellence, and value. As the saying goes, you get out of something what you put into it. Perhaps this story will illustrate this point. William Hogarth, the eminent British painter was commissioned by a tightwad millionaire to paint a story from the Old Testament. Hogarth named his price, and the millionaire proceeded to haggle until the total was about a third of what the painter wanted for doing the painting. Finally, the painter said, "Well, things have been a little slow this month; I'll go ahead and paint it for one-third of the price." Sometime later, Hogarth invited the millionaire to take a look at the finished painting. He was surprised because all he found was a huge blotch of red paint on a big white canvas. "What is it?" he asked. "The crossing of the Red Sea by the Children of Israel and the pursuit by the Egyptians," replied the painter. As he pointed to the blotch of red paint, he said, "This is the Red Sea." "Oh," said the miser, "Well, where are the Egyptians?" "They all drowned," replied the painter. "And the Israelites?" "They've all crossed over."

Service, excellence, and expertise from a trustee may not be free, but the cost will be outweighed by the value you receive and the freedom you gain to do *what you do best*. As you meet the growing challenge to remain competitive by offering new, profitable products to your customer base, selecting a good trustee may be a springboard to new markets. Good luck in your search!

NOTES

[1]These materials were prepared prior to the announcement of the two different tax law revisions proposed by the House and Senate in the Spring of 1986. Some of the issues discussed in this chapter could be impacted by the passage of either proposal, but it is impossible to forecast what revisions will be incorporated in the final bill. Therefore, after reading these materials, readers should familiarize themselves with any pertinent tax law revisions adopted after January, 1986.

Product Positioning and Marketing

Once the self-directed IRA product has been established, the question becomes one of positioning and marketing. Even a defensive strategy demands sufficient market segmentation to target appropriate customers before an institution might move elsewhere. An aggressive strategy may require calculation to get the maximum marketing results with the most efficient expenditure of marketing resources.

Kenneth Kehrer demonstrates the degree to which sophisticated product positioning and marketing can derive from market research. He has pioneered in developing an index of target efficiency, a well-conceived cross-selling technique, which asks what relationships customers currently have that may predict their predispositions toward other products and services we might offer. Understanding this technique will permit marketers to increase results by knowing they have a better than random chance of success by contacting a particular customer for a particular product.

Next we include an often neglected view, namely that of a front-line customer sales representative. Phillip Hanson has been for the past two years one of the nation's leading brokers, selling securities from within a depository institution. His comments show unique insight into management objectives gained by an insightful practitioner in one of the Southwest's premier thrifts.

As this volume was going to press, the Senate passed a tax reform bill which curtailed the universal deductibility of IRAs. The final chapter analyzes the proposed change and its possible impact on self-directed IRAs.

11. Targeting the Market for Self-Directed IRAs

THE CHANGING IRA MARKET

By June 1985, American households had over $200 billion invested in individual retirement account (IRA) and Keogh plans. IRA/Keogh assets have grown to more than five times the level they had reached when the Economic Recovery Act of 1981 attempted to encourage retirement savings by permitting households to invest in IRAs with pre-tax dollars (see Table 11.1).

As the dollar value of IRA/Keogh assets has grown, so has competition among financial services organizations for IRA/Keogh investment funds. This competition is expected to heighten as the average balances in IRAs grow through annual contributions and tax-sheltered accumulation.

The IRA market has been characterized by:

• Explosive growth
• Customer loyalty
• Dominance by banks and savings and loans
• Popularity of certificates of deposit (CDs) as IRA investment vehicles
• Use of passive investment strategies by consumers

However, important changes are occurring in the IRA market. These changes could have far-reaching effects on the competitive position of each financial services organization and on the efficacy of traditional IRA marketing strategies.

Slowing of Growth

The annual rate of growth in IRA/Keogh assets has slowed and may have stabilized, as Table 11.1 illustrates. While growth is still very high, the growth rate now appears to be fueled by the annual contributions of existing IRA account holders rather than by the growth in new IRA participants.

123

TABLE 11.1
IRA and Keogh Assets: Annual Rate of Growth

End of	Billion Dollars	Annual Growth Rate
December 1981	38.2	
December 1982	69.0	81%
December 1983	113.9	65%
December 1984	162.7	43%
June 1985	202.4	*42%

*Over June 1984

Source: *Employee Benefit Research Institute (EBRI)*

The Economic Recovery Act of 1981 liberalized the use of individual retirement accounts to encourage Americans to save for retirement. By extending the benefits of tax-free accumulation to all employees and their spouses, it was hoped that the majority of U.S. households would participate in this attractive retirement plan.

TABLE 11.2
Growth in IRA Participation

	% of All Households
1983	16%[a]
1984	21%[b]
1985	24%[c]

Sources:
[a]*Federal Reserve Board,* Survey of Consumer Finance
[b]*Life Insurance Management and Research Association*
[c]*Financial Institutions Marketing Association/Raddon Financial Group*

While IRA participation has grown, it is clearly approaching a plateau (Table 11.2). Some industry analysts do not expect IRA penetration to exceed 30 percent for several years.

In a recent survey, half of all households that have not yet funded an IRA (38 percent of all households) said that they intended to open an IRA soon (Table 11.3). We do not expect this kind of increase in IRA participation. Market surveys on consumer buying intentions tend to overstate consumer behavior, often by very wide margins. We see the interest exhibited by consumers that have not yet opened an IRA as an indication of the size of the long-run market potential, not short-run demand.

TABLE 11.3
IRA Participation July 1985

	% of All Households
IRA Investors	24%
Intend to Participate	38%
Will Not Participate	38%
	100%

Source: *Financial Institutions Marketing Association/Raddon Financial Group*

Participation will increase but not dramatically. The continuing economic recovery will encourage new IRA participation, but lower yields on the popular savings vehicle for first-time IRA contributors (CDs) will discourage participation.

Erosion of Customer Loyalty and Bank Dominance

Historically, virtually all IRA owners made their IRA contribution to the same institution each year. Customer loyalty has been strongest among credit unions, banks, and savings institutions. But there are signs that the loyalty of IRA customers is eroding.

Almost two-thirds of IRA/Keogh assets are invested through depository institutions--commercial banks, savings & loan associations, mutual savings banks, and credit unions--largely in traditional savings instruments such as certificates of deposit (Table 11.4). But banks and

TABLE 11.4
IRA and Keogh Assets: Market Shares June 1985

	Billions of Dollars	Market Share
Commercial Banks	55.9	27.6%
Savings and Loans	49.6	24.5%
Mutual Savings Banks	11.5	5.7%
Mutual Funds	31.4	15.5%
Credit Unions	12.9	6.4%
Life Insurance Companies	15.9	7.9%
Stock Brokerage Companies	25.2	12.4%
Total	202.4	100.0%

Source: *EBRI*

savings and loans have been losing market share (Table 11.5). Life insurance companies have also lost share, while credit unions, mutual funds, and stock brokerage firms have increased their market shares.

TABLE 11.5
IRA and Keogh Assets: Changes in Market Shares

	June 1984	June 1985	Change in Share	Dollar Value (Billions)
Commercial Banks	28.2%	27.6%	-0.6	-1.2
Savings and Loans	26.2%	24.5%	-1.7	-3.4
Mutual Savings Banks	6.6%	5.7%	-0.9	-1.8
Mutual Funds	13.5%	15.5%	+2.0	+4.0
Credit Unions	5.4%	6.4%	+1.0	+2.0
Life Insurance	8.5%	7.9%	-0.6	-1.2
Stock Brokerage	11.5%	12.4%	+0.9	+1.8
Total	100.0%	100.0%		

Source: *EBRI*

Deterioration of CD Yields

CDs have been the investment of choice of the IRA contributor. About half of all IRA assets are invested in CDs. In 1982, banks and savings and loans offered very attractive yields (often one point higher than non-bank alternatives) on a *government insured* investment. Banks and savings institutions overwhelmingly captured the market.

Now when individuals go to their banks to make an IRA contribution, they find much lower interest rates. To what extent will these relatively low yields accelerate the change in where IRA assets are being invested?

The Increase in Self-Directed IRAs

IRA investments have tended to be passive; individuals invested in vehicles or with institutions where the investment would be managed for them. However, as the size of IRA balances has grown, so has the use of self-directed IRAs (SDAs). Sixteen percent of all IRAs now permit individuals to manage their IRA investment portfolio from within the account, rather than require a transfer to another IRA (Table 11.6). Acceleration in the growth of SDAs will enhance the competitive position of mutual funds and securities firms in the IRA market.

TABLE 11.6
The Growth of Self-Directed IRAs

% of IRAs

1983	6%[a]
1984	10%[b]
1985	16%[b]

Sources:
[a]*Life Insurance Management and Research Association*, IRA Sweepstakes, 1984.
[b]*Nina Fleischman, "The IRA Market," Self-Directed IRAs, a conference of the Banking Law Institute, Los Angeles, California, November 18-19, 1985.*

Shift in Marketing Focus

In 1986, some sophisticated IRA competitors have shifted their marketing efforts away from

- encouraging households that have not yet funded an IRA to open an account, and
- trying to increase their share of this year's IRA deposits.

Instead, they are focusing on getting consumers to transfer their large IRA balances. Their target is the consumer with large IRA deposits in a bank or thrift. Financial institutions have reacted with defensive tactics: bonus interest programs that dilute the profitability of their IRA deposits.

In the next section, we describe a marketing strategy that financial institutions can use to go on the offensive. This approach is taken from a broader study of the strategic options for financial services organizations in the emerging IRA market.[1]

ATTRACTING COMPETITORS' IRAs: CROSS-SELLING TO EXISTING CUSTOMERS

The existence of large growing asset balances in competitors' IRA plans constitutes a major opportunity in the IRA market. Financial institutions have neglected a sound strategy for attracting these accounts: cross-selling IRA transfers and new IRA accounts to their customers who have their IRA assets invested at competitor institutions. An institution's customer base has between two and four IRAs with other financial services providers for each IRA it has with the institution. Institutions with satisfied customers can use their existing relationships with IRA households to encourage them to transfer their IRA investments.

Efficiently cross-selling to competitors' IRA customers among an institution's customer base requires identifying who they are. Few financial institutions have comprehensive information files on their customers that describe their whole investment portfolios, including the assets invested with other institutions. If statement inserts, direct mail, or telemarketing solicitations are being used, which account relationship(s) should be used to target efficiently competitors' IRAs hiding in the customer base?

Our research indicates that an institution can dramatically increase the efficiency of marketing and reduce the cost of obtaining a new account by using a targeting approach we have pioneered: using the Index of Target Efficiency to rank customer relationships for each product an institution wants to sell to its customer base.

The Index of Target Efficiency

The Index of Target Efficiency measures how a marketing approach compares with an approach that is completely untargeted. The index is computed by dividing the proportion of target households that have a particular customer relationship (e.g., a brokerage account) by the proportion of all households or customers that have that customer account.

An index equal to 1 means that soliciting that customer relationship is no more efficient than an approach to all customers or all households.

Institutions should target customer relationships or accounts where the Index of Target Efficiency is greater than 1, that is, where an institution is more likely to reach the target market than if it used a completely random approach. An index of 2 means that soliciting that account relationship is twice as likely to reach the target household as a "shotgun" approach and the cost of obtaining a new account is (probably less than) half as much as an untargeted approach.

It is surprising how many financial services organizations use marketing approaches with an index of less than one, i.e., they are less likely to reach their target than if they used a completely untargeted approach. An index of .50 means that soliciting that account relationship is only half as likely to hit the target households as an untargeted approach. In this case, the cost of obtaining a new account would be at least twice the cost of a new account when all customers are solicited.

Our targeting approach is already being used by some leading regional banks to sell IRAs.

Targeting IRA Households

We have examined the concentration of IRA customers in three sets of customer relationships:

- Traditional banking services
- Other financial services that are being offered by several kinds of financial services organizations
- Credit cards

Traditional Banking Relationships. Even though almost every household that has an IRA also has a checking account, targeting checking account customers as potential IRA customers is not a very target-efficient strategy for cross-selling IRAs to a bank's customers. The methods of direct mail solicitation or sending checking account statement stuffers to direct deposit account (DDA) customer lists are somewhat more likely to reach IRA households than a completely untargeted approach, but targeting checking accounts is much less efficient than some other strategies.

Using checking accounts to cross-sell IRAs has an Index of Target Efficiency of 1.23, i.e, a bank is 23 percent more likely to reach an IRA household by concentrating on checking account customers than if it solicited all of its customers. This is because of the fact that, even though a high proportion (97 percent) of IRA households have checking accounts, a high proportion (75 percent) of non-IRA households also have checking accounts. Dividing .97 by .79, the proportion of all households that have checking accounts, yields an Index of Target Efficiency of 1.23 (Table 11.7).

Similarly, targeting passbook savings accounts to cross-sell IRAs to bank customers who have IRAs outside the bank or thrift is somewhat target efficient (1.28), but not as efficient as cross-selling to other banking relationships. Despite the fact that households with IRAs are more likely to have a passbook savings account than a mortgage or bank card, cross-selling IRAs to a bank's or thrift's mortgage and credit card customer base is more target efficient in finding the households who have their IRAs outside the institution.

Certificates of deposit clearly have the highest target efficiency in cross-selling IRAs in banks and thrifts. Soliciting CD customers is about twice as likely to find IRA households than soliciting all bank or thrift customers.

Soliciting a bank's loan base is quite target inefficient in terms of cross-selling IRAs. A loan customer of a bank or thrift is only 60 percent as likely to have an IRA as a randomly chosen customer.

TABLE 11.7
**Using Existing Relationships to Cross-Sell
Banking Relationships**
(Percent of Households)

	IRA Households	Non-IRA Households	Target Efficiency
Checking Accounts	97%	75%	1.23
Passbook Savings	78%	58%	1.28
Mortgages	57%	33%	1.55
Bank Cards	71%	36%	1.69
Loans	5%	9%	.60
CDs	41%	17%	1.99

Other Financial Services. Money market accounts, mutual funds, trust accounts, life insurance, and stocks and bonds have become the products increasingly used by financial services organizations to diversify their offerings. Providers that have these kinds of account relationships with their customers have a marketing advantage over banks and thrifts in efficiently targeting IRA households. Tax-free mutual funds have the highest target efficiency; soliciting households that have tax-free mutual funds is more than three times as likely to reach households with IRAs than an approach to all customers (Table 11.8).

TABLE 11.8
Using Existing Relationships to Cross-Sell IRAs:
Other Financial Services
(Percent of Households)

	IRA Households	Non-IRA Households	Target Efficiency
Money Market Accounts	32%	9%	2.48
Tax-Free Mutual Funds	6%	1%	3.29
Other Mutual Funds	7%	2%	2.41
Trust Accounts	7%	4%	1.70
Life Insurance	94%	73%	1.23
Bonds	10%	2%	2.74
Stocks	28%	9%	2.33

However, cross-selling IRA transfer plans to stock brokerage and bond customers, money market accounts, and mutual fund owners is also very target efficient--more efficient than targeting any traditional banking relationship. Targeting trust account customers to sell IRA transfers is more target efficient than targeting any bank relationship other than CDs. Life insurance has an Index of Target Efficiency that is similar to checking and passbook savings accounts.

Thus, mutual funds companies and brokerage firms have an advantage over banks and thrifts and life insurance companies in cross-selling IRA transfer plans to customers who have their IRAs with other organizations. Mutual fund organizations and securities firms can target their competitors' IRAs much more efficiently, and the cost of acquiring an IRA account from a customer who has an IRA at another institution is substantially lower.

Credit Cards. Credit cards are becoming an increasingly important distribution channel in the emerging financial services industry. Each type of credit card has high target efficiency in cross-selling IRAs (Table 11.9).

Soliciting national travel/entertainment card (American Express, Diners Club, the new Sears DisCover card) and gasoline company credit card customers is more than twice as efficient as an untargeted approach. National retailer cards (Sears, Penney's, K-Mart, etc.) have somewhat lower target efficiency than bank, other store, and affinity group cards in cross-selling IRA transfers, but as a group credit cards are an efficient way to reach households that have IRAs.

TABLE 11.9
Using Existing Relationships to Cross-Sell IRAs:
Credit Cards
(Percent of Households)

	IRA Households	Non-IRA Households	Target Efficiency
Gas Cards	54%	23%	1.93
Bank Cards	71%	36%	1.69
Travel/Entertainment Cards	21%	8%	2.10
National Retailer Cards	71%	43%	1.51
Other Store Cards	62%	32%	1.68
Other Cards	10%	5%	1.67

Competing for the IRA Transfer Business

A financial services provider can efficiently market to the hidden IRAs in its customer base by targeting the customer relationships where its competitors' IRAs are concentrated. Banks and thrifts should target their CD customers. All financial services organizations should target mutual funds accounts (particularly tax-free funds) and credit card customers. Banks and thrifts have a *market advantage* over other providers in obtaining annual IRA contributions, given the large number of IRAs among CD accounts. But mutual funds and securities firms have a countervailing *market advantage*. Due to the relative concentration of IRA owners in their customer base, their marketing efficiency can be translated into lower costs of acquiring an IRA relationship.

Clearly, banks and thrifts that are registered broker/dealers or which market securities through a networking venture are well positioned to compete for the IRA transfer business. They will be able to build their SDA account base despite the vigorous competition from brokerage houses and mutual funds.

NOTES

[1]Kenneth Kehrer, *The IRA Market: Growing Opportunities for the Financial Services Industry*, (Kenneth Kehrer Associates: Princeton, 1985).

12. Selling Securities in a Financial Institution: A Practitioner's Viewpoint

Along with financial industry deregulation has come the opportunity for banks and savings and loans to expand into securities brokerage. Successfully doing so requires an understanding not only of the differences in goals, methods, and markets between banking and brokerage, but also between traditional brokerage and bank sponsored brokerage.

The case of First Texas Savings will be used throughout this chapter. First Texas has subscribed to INVEST, a service of ISFA Corp. Through the INVEST service, First Texas has available alternative investments to customers who, for whatever reason, find that CDs or other bank products do not at present meet their investment needs. Major brokerage firms and insurance companies (not to mention a few department stores) are encroaching on traditional bank territory, competing with banking institutions for the hearts and minds of retail customers. If one of our customers does seek an alternative, we prefer that he do business at First Texas rather than another brokerage firm.

Most of the business INVEST does is with First Texas customers and, as one would expect, they generally are conservative, unsophisticated investors; the majority have little or no investing experience outside CDs. Because of these factors, the principal task is in educating customers, helping them become comfortable with what are often new and intimidating concepts. Only after they understand the product, and how it meets their objectives, will they buy it.

Such education is far more effective in person than over the phone: The primary goal of prospecting calls is to sell the appointment (of course, the broker will close the sale on the phone if the opportunity arises). The branch office where the customer usually banks is the best location; the familiar surroundings put the customer at ease, reducing buying resistance. This is especially true if a large amount of money, or the customer's life savings, or both are involved.

What is the typical customer looking for in an investment? Safety is paramount. By and large the customer is in his mid 50s or older and is risk-averse, which is why he invests in bank products--he often feels that he is too old to make up any financial losses. Nevertheless, he is suffering from interest rate shock--his 13 percent CDs opened two years ago will today renew at 9 percent. He wants a high, steady return, usually in the form of monthly interest, because he is wary of the ephemera of capital appreciation. In fact, the word "stock" seems to be a strong pejorative; many customers immediately associate it with gambling.

The products INVEST sells most are high grade bond mutual funds and unit trusts. The customer prefers them because of safety and high or tax-free income. Few of our customers are, or will become, stock traders so worrying about locking up the customer's money is useless.

Approximately 55 percent of the business is in government securities mutual funds, making them far and away the most popular product INVEST offers. Customers can see similarities between these funds and CDs: high degree of safety, generally steady return, monthly interest check or compounding. Since these funds invest primarily in government securities, credit risk is easily dealt with, but overcoming the fear of market risk can be a problem. One way is to compare the fund's safety to that of everything from IBM to oil futures, all the while keeping the customer mindful of the current 200 basis point spread between fund and CD yields. The customer can then see that in the scheme of things the government fund is indeed safe.

Individual retirement accounts are a good way to attract new clients, as well as a good reason to contact existing clients for additional business. Many people have been contributing to IRAs for several years and have built up significant balances. Again, with CD yields relatively low, a rollover to a government security can be appropriate.

Another 25 percent of the business is in tax-free investments, once again primarily in mutual funds and unit trusts. Customers who are well established sometimes find themselves with high disposable income and few tax breaks. They have CDs earning taxable income they do not currently need, they resent losing so much of it to taxes, and they are ready for a change. For an individual in a 35 percent tax bracket, 8.5 percent tax-free is equivalent to 13.1 percent before taxes in a taxable investment. Where can one find a high quality taxable investment paying 13.1 percent? In these instances tax-free investments sell themselves.

Some customers willing to accept more risk go with equity products (mutual funds, of course) with returns ranging from approximately 15 percent compounded annually for the equity-income and balanced funds, to 27 percent and higher for the aggressive growth funds. Generally, these customers are between the ages of 25 and 45, and though they are willing to accept more risk they realize that the funds provide a level of diversity they cannot easily achieve investing in stocks.

Real estate limited partnerships would seem to have great potential, but so far this INVEST group has done very little in this product area. Soft real estate markets and tax reform are the principal reasons, but also the brokers seem reluctant to show partnerships to the customer. After all, the more complicated the sales pitch, the less chance of a sale, and partnerships are relatively complicated: Why not stay with a winner, such as the tax-free bond fund? One of the real estate syndicators is having a series of local seminars; perhaps listening to the limited partnership's expert will help the customer understand the advantages of this kind of investment.

Marketing efforts are done primarily through direct mail to holders of demand deposit accounts; newspaper and magazine advertising has been ineffective. First Texas has been understandably cautious about targeting CD account holders; there is the obvious concern about disintermediation, but also the branch offices are expected to maintain a positive growth in deposits.

This introduces the most effective prospecting tool: the branch employee referral. Such a referral usually means the customer had expressed an interest; perhaps he saw a sign in the branch lobby. Since a customer will seldom call the broker, it is important that the branch employee get the customer's name and phone number so the broker can call the customer. To that end, a referral incentive program has been put in place which rewards the branch employee for each account opened. The result has been a stream of generally well-qualified leads and a very high closing ratio.

The reason First Texas subscribed to INVEST was to generate profits. As with many other highly leveraged businesses, a compromise has to be found between the goals of generating maximum revenues and controlling expenses. For example, if a firm has monthly expenses of, say $50,000 and makes $60,000 in one month, it has a profit of $10,000; if the next month revenues are $70,000, the firm has doubled its profit on a 16.67 percent increase in revenue. Equivalently, if the firm again makes $60,000 but cuts expenses to $40,000, profit has once again doubled.

To help control expenses, the INVEST program at First Texas uses a hub and spoke structure. In the Dallas area, all of the brokers are in the First Texas corporate headquarters, with each responsible for several branch offices trying to create rapport with branch personnel and developing the branch as a referral source. As mentioned previously, appointments with customers are generally at the branch offices; a broker might visit several branches on any given day.

This structure not only reduces expenses (secretarial help, office supplies, leasing office space, etc.), it aids the flow of ideas and information, and engenders a spirit of competition and camaraderie.

Using a securities brokerage operation to complement the traditional banking structure requires an awareness of competing interests and prejudices.

The securities business is by nature hectic, pressured, and preoccupied with immediate results; the brokers are correspondingly aggressive. Some employees of the banking side disapprove of this and, further, resent the intrusion into their areas; indeed, many have difficulty understanding why securities brokerage services are offered at all.

By the same token, the brokerage people must understand the banking side's goals, methods, and pressures, especially with regard to liability account production. Attention must be paid to how much money the brokerage side is taking out of the institution. Branch and regional people have considerable autonomy and cannot, for example, be compelled to refer customers. The brokers must be able to work within that structure.

The brokerage side should be managed much like a traditional brokerage firm aggressively pursuing business with brokers being paid in proportion to their production, etc., but with special awareness of the following facts:

- The majority of customers are conservative, long term investors; they are not, nor are likely ever to be, stock traders.
- The brokerage side's relationship with branch and regional level bank employees is often delicate.

Successfully combining securities brokerage with bank resources requires commitment, communication, and a willingness to experiment; the potential rewards of doing so, however, are tremendous.

13. Tax Reform and the Future of IRA Marketing

As this book was being prepared for publication, the Senate Finance Committee sent tax reform legislation to the full Senate which called for returning the IRA to its 1981 status. The bill was passed by the Senate with a non-binding resolution calling for the House/Senate Conference Committee to restore IRA deductions as long as the top tax rates were not thereby increased. Essentially, the proposed legislation called for eliminating deductible IRA contributions for those covered in pension plans. Workers in this category could continue to contribute to IRAs, but only with after-tax dollars. Accumulation of IRA dollars once contributed would continue to be on a tax-deferred status.

Several arguments were raised to support this position. IRA contributors have disproportionately come from the upper income brackets. As reported by Market Facts in its 1986 IRA market survey, 35 percent of IRA contributors have incomes in excess of $40,000; the average income of the IRA contributor is $36,000. The average income for the population as a whole is considerably lower, $24,000. Forty percent of IRA contributors have a net worth in excess of $100,000 with the average net worth of the IRA contributor being $131,000, approximately double that of the non-contributor ($58,000).

Detractors painted the IRA as a vehicle for the relatively wealthy, suggesting the program belonged more truly in the classification of a tax shelter than in a broad-based retirement planning option.

Additionally the argument was heard that permitting participation in both an IRA and a pension program represented a tax advantaged form of "double-dipping." To lower the top brackets and produce a "revenue neutral" bill, an either/or choice between IRAs and pension plans seem to some a reasonable limitation of benefits.

While at this writing the outcome of the debate remains to be decided, the action of the Senate Finance Committee has drawn heated attention to the value of the IRA in its present form and the wisdom of the proposed limitation.

137

HOW WIDESPREAD IS IRA PARTICIPATION?

Polemics frequently are formed when the side of statistics are stressed favoring particular arguments. To note that 35 percent of the population contributing to IRAs have incomes of $40,000 or more also reveals that 65 percent have incomes under $40,000. To point out that 40 percent of IRA contributors have net worths exceeding $100,000 leaves unnoticed that 50 percent have net worths less than that amount. These statistics would suggest more broad-based participation than was initially argued.

Approximately 28 million American households, about 1/3 of all U.S. households, have already established IRAs, a number considerably in excess of the affluent, regardless of how the affluent is segmented and quantified. Surprisingly, 18% of IRA contributors had net worths less than $20,000, and 30% had net worths less than $50,000 according to the same Market Facts, Inc., survey. Market Facts itself was projecting that 40% of all U.S. households would own IRAs once 1985 contributions had been made. As shown in Figure 13.1 IRA participation has increased steadily since 1982.

FIGURE 13.1

IRA Participation

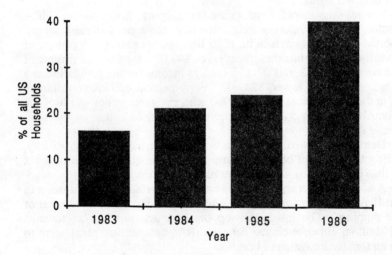

Year

Clearly, the ability to deduct $2,000 from gross income before determining net taxable income is a benefit to most taxpayers. Proportionately, however, the limited cap of $2,000 on a deductible individual contribution is actually of greater impact when the gross income from which the deduction is taken is smaller. Stated another way, the truly wealthy would probably be better advised to look beyond the IRA to reduce their taxable incomes significantly.

Granted, IRA participation by the lower income brackets has lagged. The more completely living expenses consume available discretionary income, the narrower the latitude for savings of any kind. But the IRA "wall" of about 35 percent of the population who participate demands more subtle analysis.

Initial marketing has in some instances conveyed a misleading impression that the IRA contribution must be made in one lump sum. For many people, the writing of a $2,000 check may be an experience limited to the purchase of a home or a car. Others have wondered what will happen to their initial deposits if in subsequent years they must forgo an annual contribution.

IRA marketing has not communicated the fact that contributions below the maximum are perfectly acceptable. Nor have financial intermediaries clearly communicated to IRA depositors the true impact of early withdrawal charges.

Overall, IRA marketing has been fairly unimaginative, generally stressing the tax advantage of the maximum contribution while limiting competitive positioning to matters of rate and convenience alone.

Easily, the potential depositor could mistakenly conclude that the IRA opportunity was one that demanded every April the repeated deposit of a relatively large lump sum untouchable until retirement.

Bank marketers have a responsibility to communicate more completely and in simple language that can be readily understood by all the facts that a person can contribute to an IRA in small amounts, that contributions can be made at any time of the year in varying amounts and that the total amount contributed in a year can be less than the maximum contribution.

So, too, must we communicate the actual impact of penalties if a person needs to use IRA deposits prior to age 59-1/2. Granted, the penalties will reduce the yield, but for many depositors their only source of cash available in an emergency is their IRA. In those cases, an early withdarawl penalty may mean less interest or no interest, but at least the principal may be available for return intact.

Of all the IRA marketers, the credit unions have been the most successful in reaching middle income Americans. As shown in Figure 13.2, between 1982 and 1985, the IRA market share commanded by credit unions has increased nearly 1.75 times percentage-wise and 10.75 times in absolute dollar amounts. In 1985, credit unions commanded nearly $14 billion in IRA deposits.

FIGURE 13.2

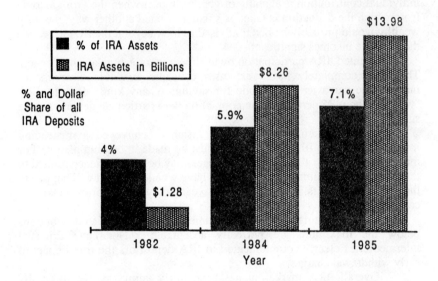

Perhaps these results suggest the degree to which credit unions have pioneered in payroll deduction IRAs, whereby an individual worker can select an automatic amount of each paycheck deposited to the IRA. Here, a person may start with a modest amount, perhaps as little as $10.00 each pay period, in a starter IRA geared to match income and expense ratios more easily accessible. Moreover, with the automatic deduction a person can budget, calculating living expenses on the amount remaining after the IRA savings. In the worker's spending psychology, the dollars were never received hence they were not as easily missed.

As marketers, we have not appreciated the importance of systematic and budgeted savings. During World War II very few were able to afford the purchase of complete war bonds, but millions were sold to people of modest means who bought pieces of bonds at their places of employment.

Interestingly, when Market Facts surveyed the potential IRA market, those who had not yet contributed, automatic deduction was seen as one of the most likely techniques to attract new depositors. As shown in Figure 13.3, one-half of all potential IRA owners expressed interest in this approach.

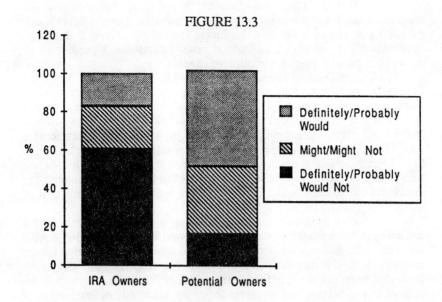

FIGURE 13.3

Disproportionate IRA participation by the more affluent among us may simply be an effect of initial adoption and early marketing, not a bias in the IRA *per se*.

HOW ADEQUATE ARE PENSION PROGRAMS AS RETIREMENT SAVINGS PLANS?

The Senate Finance Committee's version of tax reform would lower from 10 years to 5 years the employment period required for vesting benefits. The Employee Benefit Research Institute, an industry lobbying group supporting work-related benefit programs, embraced this alternative as a means to extend the base of retirement coverage more than retaining the deductible IRA contribution would. Clearly, anyone favoring the development of retirement savings would applaud the efforts to strengthen pension coverage. Still, the question remains whether the trade-off is sound public policy.

IRAs differ from pension programs, but they resemble 401(k) plans in that individuals can contribute their earned dollars in a manner where those dollars remain totally within the individual's control. Both the IRA and the 401(k) require trust administration independent of the employer. Defined benefit and defined contribution pension plans generally are administered by the employer and typically are dependent upon the employer for their status and continuance.

The first difficulty with pension programs is that they can be terminated, and terminations generally reduce the benefit level paid. According to statistics kept by the Employee Benefit Research Institute, approximately 3 percent of all defined benefit plans and 2 percent of all defined contribution plans are terminated annually.

The Handbook of Pension Statistics, 1985, published by Commerce Clearinghouse, reports that since the passage of ERISA an estimated 4 percent of participants in defined benefit plans were affected by plan terminations. Approximately 85% of these plan terminations involve "sufficient" plans by ongoing firms, plans in which employees receive vested benefits even if the benefit levels are considerably below what would have been received under a continued plan. Further, only 48% of the participants in sufficient terminated plans worked for firms that intended to establish new (usually defined contribution or profit sharing) plans in their stead.

The economic reasons for a company's decision to terminate a sufficient pension plan include the trend toward replacing defined benefit programs with defined contribution plans which bear less obligation for the employer to fund a specified benefit level. Furthermore, corporations have been able to secure tax benefits by reversions of funds, i.e., a return to the corporation of excess pension assets above the actuarially determined level needed to fund the benefits defined.

Regardless of the reasons, workers in terminated plans suffer real losses. The Commerce Clearinghouse study referred to above estimates that worker losses in ongoing firms with sufficient terminated plans from 1979 to 1984 amounted to $4.6 billion. This amount is relatively small, representing one-half of one percent of the estimated present value of liabilities in all defined benefit plans (approximately $750 billion in 1981). But the impact on an individual worker can be severe. For each $100 of real pension benefits anticipated based on service to date, workers can expect to lose $45 as an immediate result of the plan termination. The bite of this loss is aggravated when the reason for the plan termination was reversion of excess pension assets to the corporation, not to the workers themselves.

Following ERISA, Congress established the Pension Benefit Guaranty Corporation (PBGC) to assume obligations when insufficient plans were terminated. In its first 10 years of existence, the PBGC covered nearly 1,100 terminated plans. At the beginning of 1985, the PBGC was reported to be $400 million short of the amount needed to pay retirees. Nor did the problem ease. In the last few months of 1985, the obligations of the PBGC nearly doubled.

While workers in plans assumed by the PBGC could expect to receive benefits, the payment is dependent on the Treasury. Viewed this way, ERISA did encourage private retirement savings by strengthening private pension programs. But for insufficient plans which are terminated, the ultimate obligation, as in Social Security, is once again public.

Moreover, a worker excluded from making deductible IRA contributions because of inclusion in an employer sponsored pension program is placed at a potential disadvantage. The Senate Finance Committee's tax reform proposal would prohibit such a worker from making deductible IRA contributions during the years the plan was in existence. Since we cannot predict accurately which plans will be terminated, a worker in a current plan has no way to hedge the bet that the plan might ultimately be terminated. This is especially salient, given the estimate by the Investment Company Institute that 70 to 75 percent of the 28.5 million households with IRAs are also covered by a pension plan.

Nor is reducing the vesting period to five years a dependable solution. According to a 1983 Department of Labor report on job tenure released by the Bureau of Labor Statistics, only 39.6 percent of all workers remain on their jobs over five years. Ironically, if a shorter vesting period actually achieved the desired effect of including more workers, the resulting actuarial burden on existing defined benefit plans might actually trigger increased plan terminations.

ARE TAX INCENTIVES NEEDED TO STIMULATE PRIVATE RETIREMENT SAVINGS?

An underlying impulse behind tax reform seems to be an argument that tax preferences to accomplish social goals are suspect. The argument has not been consistently advanced in the Senate Finance Committee's proposed legislation. With the IRA, for instance, tax-deferred accumulation has been retained even for those in pension programs who would have to contribute to their IRAs with after-tax dollars. For the Senate Finance Committee reformers, this retained advantage seemed an adequate incentive to stimulate continued IRA contributions.

David Silver, President of the Investment Company Institute, released a May 1986 study conducted by Market Facts, Inc., which surveyed 800 IRA owners after the proposed limits on the IRA emerged from the Senate Finance Committee. Of those surveyed, 78 percent acknowledged that the tax deduction they received for an IRA contribution was a significant incentive for making the contribution. Furthermore, two-thirds of those surveyed said they had not regularly saved before the IRA participation rules were liberalized.

As quoted in the *American Banker* of May 22, 1986, David Silver made the point that "Americans who want to save for retirement respond when given an incentive to do so." He went on to note that "Soon our ever-growing population of retirees will begin withdrawing money from their IRAs, paying taxes as they withdraw, and helping the country cope with the increased demands on the Social Security system. It seems shortsighted to take away a program that will help them save for their retirement."

To remove the tax deductibility of IRA contributions is to give the IRA no particular advantage whatsoever. Annuities by comparison also have tax-deferred internal build-up. Unlike the IRA, however, the annuity is not limited with regard to the maximum amount of after-tax dollars a person can invest. Nor are annuities saddled with the mandatory withdrawal rules inherent to the IRA when the IRA contributor reaches the age of 70-1/2.

Private retirement savings with after-tax dollars has always been possible. Even before Social Security was created to fill the void of the then virtually non-existent retirement income, after-tax savings for retirement was a possibility. Returning IRAs to their 1981 tax status may return IRAs to their 1981 contribution levels as well. Regardless of our attitudes toward tax incentives, the evidence of the IRA since 1982 is that the incentives in this case have worked remarkably well.

A Market Facts study commissioned by the Investment Company Institute estimated that $14 billion of the dollars contributed in 1983 and $18 billion in 1984 would otherwise have been spent, not saved. By 1990, the additional savings stimulated by the IRA were estimated at $50 billion annually.

Moreover, the IRA cannot be considered a true tax shelter in which income is permanently removed from tax consequences because when the savings are drawn out at retirement they are taxed. The IRA properly viewed, is not a tax shelter but actually a program in the spirit of tax reform itself. IRA savings encourage self-reliance, capital formation, and the growth of the private economy.

HOW WILL THE PROPOSED CHANGES AFFECT SELF-DIRECTED IRAs?

Self-directed IRAs currently constitute approximately 16 percent of all IRA accounts. This has been a growing market segment, projected by Market Facts to constitute a 20 percent market share when the statistics for 1985 contributions are finally calculated.

Curiously, in the debate regarding the tax status of IRAs, banks have been relatively silent. Some have speculated that the banks have stayed out of the IRA controversy because they seek primarily to preserve favorable tax treatment of bank reserves.

As the articles in this volume have made abundantly clear, banks have been losing IRA market share. With the declining interest rates of 1985 and the bull market in full stride, certificates of deposit were less attractive to IRAs than had earlier been the case. Privately, many bankers will admit that IRA deposits are high cost funds which, contrary to their initial assumptions, are not stable or long term sources of liquidity. Rather, as the 1985 tax season has made abundantly clear, even IRA funds already on deposit in banks are subject to disintermediation in favor of more competitive investment opportunities.

145

The most vocal champion in the battle for the IRA has been the mutual fund industry--the clear winner in the recent surge toward self-direction. In a sense, a mutual fund IRA is an intrinsic form of diversification if the investment goes into a family of funds which permits easy movement between different funds within the family. Even within bank-provided self-directed accounts, the inclusion of mutual funds on the investment menu alongside certificates of deposit has been an easy first step.

If IRAs were to return to their 1981 tax status, self-directed IRAs may be the only form of the account which makes any sense at all. Clearly, the population not participating in pension plans could continue to make annual tax-deductible IRA contributions, but the dollar volume of the activity would have to await rollover deposits from matured vested pension settlements. As the dollar size of the assets to be invested increases, diversification becomes not merely a prudent strategy, but virtually a required strategy. Pension funds rolled into IRAs for continued tax-deferred appreciation certainly meet the profile of the investment mix intrinsic to the self-directed account.

It is desirable that Congress not take a step that will reverse established policy by forcing the retirement savings issue once again onto the grounds of public responsibility. Surely the deductibility of contributions will be less taxing than ultimate retirement burdens which might appreciate given the limitations of pension programs and the reduced stimulus to save. But regardless of the ultimate outcome of the issue in the tax reform debate, the future looks promising for the self-directed account.

Clearly, we must emphasize that the IRA was never intended as a poverty program. But as a personal retirement savings vehicle for workers, the program has been enormously successful. In 1981, the year before IRAs were universally available, IRA assets were $25 billion. In four short years, those assets have increased more than tenfold to exceed $250 billion. Compared to most pension plans, the IRA is a program the worker keeps, regardless of place of employment or length of employment. Compared to most 401(k) plans, the IRA permits an individually determined investment not limited to the investment menu of the particular qualified plan in which the worker's company participates.

The IRA in its self-directed form permits a person to create within his or her own means a personal tax-deferred retirement investment portfolio. For many Americas this may be their major lifetime opportunity to participate in the private investment strategies generally available only to the affluent.

The elimination of the tax deductible IRA available to all workers regardless of their pension fund status would reverse with little explanation and even less reason a message Americans were given only four years ago: Take your retirement savings into your own hands and make it work for you.

About the Contributors

JEROME R. CORSI, editor of this volume, serves as senior vice president, bank marketing, at Marketing One Inc., a firm which specializes in developing insurance and securities sales delivery systems for depository institutions. Other recent professional experience includes: president, Benemax Incorporated; vice president, bank marketing, Benefit Concepts of America; and director of market research and new product development, The MacGruder Agency. Dr. Corsi received his B.A. from Case Western Reserve University in Cleveland, Ohio, where he majored in political science and economics and earned his Ph.D. from the Harvard University Department of Government. He is a registered principal with the National Association of Securities Dealers.

FINANCIAL SERVICES GROUP is a division of *Market Facts, Inc.,* the largest publicly-held research firm in the U.S. The group was formed in order to meet the specialized marketing research needs of the financial services industry. Syndicated reports are published on the market for a variety of financial products, including recently: *The IRA Marketplace, Mutual Funds '86,* and *Discount Brokerage: Update '86.*

JERRY L. FITZWATER is vice president and senior trust officer in Union Bank's Institutional Trust Services Department, where he is currently involved in sales and marketing activities. He has been a frequent speaker on retirement plan topics. Mr. Fitzwater graduated from California State University, Los Angeles, with a degree in economics. He is also affiliated with the Braille Institute of America, Inc., where he serves as a director and a member of the executive committee, and is chairman of the institute's retirement plan committee.

PHILLIP HANSON, educated at the University of Kansas, has consistently been one of the top producers in the First Texas Savings INVEST program since its inception nearly two years ago. He is also executive vice president of Hanson Financial, a private marketing firm, and Hanson Development, a private investment firm. Prior to joining First Texas Savings, Mr. Hanson was supervisor of a project with the Treasury Department for a Washington, D.C., area consulting firm.

KENNETH C. KEHRER, president, Kenneth Kehrer Associates, is a leading authority on consumer financial services behavior and on the consumer business strategies of banks, thrifts, insurance companies, and securities brokerage firms. Dr. Kehrer has provided expert testimony to both houses of Congress, most recently to the Senate Banking Committee, where he was the central witness on hearings on deregulation. He has published numerous articles on banking, insurance, securities, and IRAs. Prior to forming Kenneth Kehrer Associates, he was a principal of Mathematica, a Princeton-based software, research, and consulting organization. He holds a Ph.D. in economics from Yale University and has nearly 20 years of experience in information systems, surveys and market research.

GERALD KERNS is president, CEO, and secretary of Marketing One Securities, Inc. Prior to joining Marketing One Securities, Mr. Kerns was associated with the IRA Institute in Portland, Oregon, and was vice president of Far West Federal Bank. Mr. Kerns is a graduate of Notre Dame University.

CONNIE L. MATSUI managed marketing, customer services, and operations for Wells Fargo's retirement programs divison. Prior to joining the division in 1982, she worked in the bank's retail branch system and the central marketing group. She joined Wells Fargo in 1977 after receiving her M.B.A. degree in marketing and finance from Stanford University.

MARY L. MOHR is president of First Retirement Marketing, Inc., an affiliate of First Trust Corporation. She holds advanced degrees in law and business from the University of Denver and earned her B.A. degree at Gettysburg College. Ms. Mohr is a board member of First Trust Corporation and the Denver Chamber Orchestra.

ELIZABETH J. JOHNSTON-O'CONNOR conducts primary consumer behavior and marketing resources research on life insurance and related financial products for LIMRA. Previously a human resources consultant for Xerox Corporation, she joined LIMRA in 1980 as an associate scientist. Dr. Johnston-O'Connor is a graduate of St. Bonaventure University and received her M.A. and Ph.D. degrees from the University of Rochester.

RADDON FINANCIAL GROUP is a Chicago-based full service marketing consulting firm that specializes in financial service firms. It works with over three hundred organizations across the country representing the banking, savings institutions, securities, insurance, real estate, and credit union industries. Twice a year the Raddon Financial Group does national consumer research that tracks changes in the financial services market and identifies trends for profitability.

DAVID C. SHELTON is a partner in The Winchester Law Firm where his practice involves the representation of financial institutions and financial services providers throughout the nation. His practice also deals with all aspects of financial institution representation, including formation of new institutions, formation and utilization of bank holding companies, acquisitions, and mergers, as well as product development and expansion. He lectures and participates frequently in banking and savings and loan related programs. Mr. Shelton received his undergraduate and law degrees from Memphis State University.

PAUL A. WERLIN, senior vice president of investment services, ISFA Corporation, manages the insurance, research, asset management, financial planning, and sales assistance departments. These departments provide the INVEST network with investment products and recommendations, professional services, and technical support. Before joining ISFA Corporation as a vice president and regional director in 1982, Mr. Werlin served as assistant manager of the Madison Avenue branch of E.F. Hutton & Company in New York City. He received his M.B.A. in finance from New York University, holds a New York and Florida state insurance license, is a general securities principal, a registered options principal, and a municipal securities principal.

Index

ABA. *See* American Bankers
    Association
ABA Retail Deposit services, 9
Accounting systems, 87, 112
Add-to options, 76
Administration, 117
    fees, 115–116
    trust accounts, 107, 109–110
Advertising, 9, 17–18, 22, 42–43,
    96, 104, 129, 135
    Washington Mutual, 77–78
Advisory services, 95
Aggressive growth equity fund, 17
American Bankers Association
    (ABA), 60–61
Annual fees, 115–116
Annual reports, 113–114
Annuities, 3, 44, 52–53, 73(table)
    investment distribution, 28,
    29(fig.), 33(table), 34(table)
    in IRAs, 69, 74
    tax deferment, 143, 144
Assets, 101–102
    growth, 123–127
    Washington Mutual, 79–80
    Wells Fargo Bank, 81, 87
Autonomy, 88

Back-loaded products, 67
Balanced funds, 13
BankCal. *See* Bank of California
Bank cards, 129. *See also* Credit
    cards

"Banker's Choice" plans, 17
Bank Holding Company Act, 54
Bank of Beverly Hills, 117
Bank of California (BankCal), N.A.,
    57, 58, 59
Bank of San Diego, 118
Banks, 3, 7, 10(table), 11
    broker/dealers, 68(fig.), 85
    investment diversification, 3, 11
    investment restrictions, 14, 16
    IRA deposits, 1–2, 26, 27
    market share, 9, 43(fig.)
    mutual funds, 13, 14, 15(table),
    16, 17, 18
Basic Retirement Plan, 99. *See also*
    Keogh accounts
Benefit Service Corporation, 76
Blue chip funds, 20
Bond funds, 15
Bonds, 3, 13, 85, 103, 130
Brokerages, 19, 41(table)
    full-service, 26, 27(fig.), 28(table),
    31(table), 32(table)
    independent discount, 27(fig.),
    28(table), 31(table), 32(table)
    IRA competition, 3, 9, 11
    IRA investments, 26, 27(fig.),
    28(table), 31(table), 32(table), 85
    market share, 43(fig.), 125(table),
    126
    self-directed accounts, 2–3
    See also Broker/dealerships;
    Discount brokerages

151

156